AF480670

THIS WE BELIEVE

FOUNDATIONAL DOCTRINES OF BASIC BIBLE TRUTH

HOWARD G. TADLOCK

BOUNLESS HORIZON
PUBLISHING

To my children-
James G.
Sharon
Bonita
Ricky

FOREWORD

While reading the manuscript of *This We Believe,* written by the Reverend Howard G. Tadlock, I sensed that this was a work developed to meet an important need in Christian living — that is the need to be ready always to give an answer to every man that asketh you a reason for the hope that is in you ... We must know what we believe... Someone has said, "Stand for something or you might fall for anything."

There is no excuse for ignorance in an enlightened and educated age. It is not enough to believe; to know what we believe is equally important. The need for such a book as *This We Believe is* found in the individual, in the church and in the movement. Therefore, I am pleased to be privileged to present the foreword to This *We Believe* written by the Reverend Howard G. Tadlock.

Brother Tadlock is a personal friend and fellow minister in the faith. He has applied himself in a scholarly manner, as well as developing himself practically to meet the demands of his calling. After he finished his Master's program he took up his pen to complete what I understand will be his first work in book form.

He enjoys a full proof ministry as a successful pastor, a church administrator and the father of a successful pastor. His years of rich experience seem to surface in his writings. From these writings, I am confident, a catalog of material will be developed which will greatly assist Christian workers and church leaders. His work is well documented and easy to understand. This enhances its potential for a wide area of use.

I extend my personal commendations to this man who, though extremely busy as a pastor of a growing church, has taken time to upgrade his ministry and then apply what he has learned by reproducing it in written form.

May God bless the author, the book and you — the reader.

   - Roy M. Chappell, D.D.
   General Superintendent
   Pentecostal Church of God

LEGACY THAT MATTERS

After a lifetime of clergy ministry my devout father left me no monetary inheritance. Like Paul the Apostle who supported himself as a tentmaker and as so many other dedicated ministers have done to support themselves in God's great church labor of love, my dad also worked extra jobs to keep himself in his ministry calling. Yes, he left me no monetary inheritance but nevertheless he did leave me a LEGACY THAT MATTERS, a legacy of faith. He imparted that faith into my life. In personal conversations, through teaching, preaching, influence, especially his example in relation-ships of caring for people who at times didn't treat him fairly, which was not unusual in his profession. I recall as a young PK(preacher's kid) sincerely asking my dad on occasions how do you take that mistreatment, he would always give me the same scriptural answer which was imparted into my spirit, 'vengeance is mine saith the lord, I will repay'. Now that I am older and wiser through his example I understand the value and discernment gained by following Bible truth in Pentecostal power. Dad never claimed he was perfect and I am not saying that he was perfect but simply to gratefully give honor to whom honor is due.

At my dad's celebration of life service in the church I have pastored for thirty-four years, I was asked by family to officiate and my response was to my younger brother Rick who had been diagnosed with cancer and died himself just three months later, asking I will officiate but I want you to team up with me and we will preach the service together, he did and that is another blessed story in itself of our legacy we shared together.

The Message God gave me for that service was entitled "WE HAVE THIS TREASURE ". In 2 Corinthians 4:7 it says, "But we have this treasure in earthen vessels, that the excellency of the power may be of God, and not of us".

It was not necessary to go into detail and really is it ever regarding "earthen vessel" issues? Except enough information to testify of God's redeeming grace and give all the glory to Him. You see the treasure is not about our sin but the treasure is about the good news of what we call the full gospel of grace that Jesus provided at great sacrifice to whosoever will call upon the name of the Lord.

Dad preached the gospel and left me, my family and this world with a treasure of which wealth, fame or power can never obtain but only through the precious blood of Calvary's lamb slain from the foundation of this world for our sin that we might have this priceless treasure now in earthen vessels and throughtout eternity, fully redeemed.

My dad left me with a legacy that matters, he even wrote it down and made it plain to read in a book entitled, THIS WE BELIEVE. Here it is republished to help you build your own life legacy that truly matters more than anything .

When all is said and done, in the end it's not what we say about each other or think of ourselves but what God thinks and says of us that really matters.

I love you dad and miss you but rejoice greatly in the greatest treasure of all which is to have something sent from God to believe in which transforms life and lasts forever.

    Your grateful son,
    - James G. (Jim) Tadlock, D.D.

Drs. Howard G. Tadlock & James G. Tadlock, praying together

APPRECIATION

To the many ministers who have asked for copies of this book only to be disappointed that it was no longer in print and to those who have encouraged me to republish my dad's book,

To my son Mike who offered to use his valuable experience in publishing his own books to republish his grandfather's printed legacy,

To my wife Brenda, sons Kevin and Darin for their love and care for dad in the last years of his life and finally,

To my dad with love for his devotion and faithful ministry as men's ministry leader for several years in Visalia New Life Church where I have pastored for thirty-four years. To the very end of his ministry on earth, dad believed what he wrote and blessed us with a legacy of faith that is shared for others to enjoy with benefits that will last eternally.

I am truly grateful and forever blessed!

- Jim Tadlock

PREFACE/ ACKNOWLEDGMENT

This series of doctrinal studies was first prepared in note form, to be taught in the author's Bible class, at the church where he pastored for fifteen and one-half years.

The response from the class was gratifying, as well as comments from visiting fellow ministers; some have said that this series should be taught in all churches. The author being aware of the need for doctrinal teaching, recommends that this series be taught as an elective in Pentecostal Sunday schools, as well as Evangelical churches.

This series would be excellent for the new members class. The author has sought to write so that this series could be taught to teen-agers, as well as juniors. Also with enough depth that a pastor could use this material to teach to his church in a midweek service.

My prayer goes with this work that God will bless all who read it. That through the study of these pages the student will come to know better what he believes and why he believes it. May God who loves you establish you in the faith of His eternal truth.

- Howard G. Tadlock, Ph.D.

To my wife Mary S. Tadlock, who typed and helped edit the manuscript. I shall ever be grateful for her help which was tremendous value to me. Without her support, I could never have finished this work.

ABOUT THE AUTHOR

Doctor Howard G. Tadlock was born November 16, 1927, and was promoted to heaven On June 20, 2020. He was ordained to the ministry in 1954 with the Pentecostal Church of God. He attended Pentecostal Bible College. He earned degrees from the California Graduate School of Theology (Th.B., M.A.), the International Bible Institute and Seminary (Th.D.), and the School of Bible Theology (Ph.D.).During more than six decades of ministry, Reverend Tadlock faithfully pastored churches across California, serving in leadership on the official boards of all three California Districts of the Pentecostal Church of God. He was the longtime pastor of the Pentecostal Church of God in Norwalk, California, beginning in 1969, and later served as Dean of Crossroads Institute of Theology in Westminster, California. After semi-retireing in Visalia, California he ministered as guest speaker in various churches and assisted his son, "Pastor Jim" at Visalia New Life Church until his heavenly homegoing.

Reverend Tadlock was deeply respected for his teaching, compassion, and lifelong dedication to spreading the Gospel. His ministry continues to inspire through his writings and the many lives he has touched.

CONTENTS

STATEMENT OF FAITH

This we believe . . .

In the verbal inspiration of the Scriptures, both the Old and New Testaments.

Our God is a trinity in unity, manifested in three persons: the Father, the Son, and the Holy Ghost.

In the deity of our Lord Jesus Christ, in His virgin birth, in His sinless life, in His miracles, in His vicarious and atoning death on the cross, in His bodily resurrection, in His ascension to the right hand of the Father, and in His personal return in power and glory.

That regeneration by the Holy Ghost for the salvation of lost and sinful man, through faith in the shed blood of Jesus Christ, is absolutely essential.

In a life of holiness, without which no man can see the Lord, through sanctification as a definite, yet progressive work of grace.

In the Baptism of the Holy Ghost, received subsequent to the new birth, with the speaking in other tongues, as the Spirit gives utterance, as the initial physical sign and evidence.

In water baptism by immersion for believers only, which is a direct commandment of our Lord, in the Name of the Father, and of the Son, and of the Holy Ghost.

In the Lord's supper and washing of the saints' feet.

That divine healing is provided for in the atonement, and is available to all who truly believe.

In the premillennial second coming of Jesus: first, to resurrect the righteous dead and to catch away the living saints to meet Him in the air; and, second, to reign on the earth a thousand years.

In the bodily resurrection of both the saved and the lost: they that are saved unto the resurrection of life, and they that are lost unto the resurrection of damnation.

INTRODUCTION

In this series "This We Believe" we will deal with some of the major doctrines of the Bible. These are considered to be the fundamentals of our faith. This statement of faith is accepted by most Pentecostal believers as well as many Evangelicals.

What we think about when the term doctrinal teaching is used, is the teaching of Church beliefs. It is that, but of more importance, doctrinal teaching is the teaching of Bible truth. The Bible is to be our main textbook, as, "All scripture is given by inspiration of God, and is profitable for doctrine, for reproof, for correction, for instruction in righteousness" (2 Timothy 3:16).

This is not to say that all teaching of church beliefs is wrong. The teaching of church belief should never violate Scripture. A church can set standards without violating Scripture. Some examples would be: age limits for church membership, particular dress for choir and certain standards for church leadership. There could be many other things added to this list. Some of this teaching is good, but can be wrong if it isn't examined in the teaching of Bible truth.

There is a lot of teaching today in churches that is only church tradition. Much of this teaching of church tradition is without any Bible basis. Jesus spoke of this condition when He said, "But in vain they do worship me, teaching for doctrine the commandments of men" (Matthew 15:9).

There is a need for doctrinal teaching in the church today. Teaching of Bible doctrine is vital to the spiritual life of a church. Paul speaking to Titus says, "Holding fast the faithful word as he hath been taught, that he may be able by sound doctrine both to exhort and to convince the gainsay-ers" (Titus 1:9).

Doctrinal teaching gives foundation to the church. Paul writes to the Ephesian church that they "…they henceforth be no more children, tossed to and fro, and carried about with every wind of doctrine, by the sleight of men, and cunning craftiness, whereby they lie in wait to deceive" (Ephesians 4:14).

Doctrinal teaching produces unity in the church. The church should be "Endeavoring to keep the unity of the Spirit in the bond of peace" (Ephesians 4:3).

Doctrinal teaching will project a good testimony for the church. "…that ye all speak the same thing, and that there be no divisions among you; but that ye be perfectly joined together in the same mind and in the same judgment" (1 Corinthians 1:10).

CHAPTER 1
THE INSPIRATION OF SCRIPTURE

The Scriptures of the Old and New Testaments are the inspired Word of God (2 Timothy 3:16) presenting to us the complete revelation of His will for the salvation of man, and constituting the Divine and only rule of Christian faith and practice (2 Peter 1:21).

We refer to the Scripture as the Word of God, also the Holy Bible. The Bible is a miracle book. Before we go into our discussion of inspiration on Scripture, let it be said that it is another of God's miracles. We do not know how God could take fallible man and produce an infallible book. The Scripture bears the stamp of its Author; even though we cannot explain how He did it.

To say Scripture is inspired is to say it is, "God breathed." According to Myer Pearlman, inspiration is defined as, "the supernatural influence of the Spirit of God on the human mind, by which prophets and apostles and sacred writers were qualified to set forth Divine truth without any mixture of error." This we believe: all Scripture is Divine truth and without error. No part of the Scripture came into being by the "will of man." It is of Divine source. "Holy men of God spake" (2 Peter 1:21).

The Bible is the most wonderful book in all the world. A student of the Bible will be quick to see it is not like any other book. It is read more than any other book, it is loved as well as hated. The student of Scripture must settle in his mind that the Bible is entirely from God — that the Bible speaks for itself and that man's theories are unacceptable. We will consider a few of these theories.

The Natural Theory

The natural theory of inspiration holds that all men are divinely inspired because God dwells in all men. On the basis of creation, man partakes of the nature of God. Therefore there is a spark of divinity in every man. The difference in degree of inspiration is explained on the basis of natural and mental capacities, or spiritual powers. In this theory, inspiration varies according to the degree of human faculties and capacities. This view would include Shakespeare, Emerson, Carlyle, as well as Isaiah, John, and Paul. There is no support in the Bible for this view in its main contention. We believe there are no degrees of inspiration; all the Bible is equally inspired, that is, equally authoritative and true.

The Illumination Theory

This theory believes that all Christians possess the gift of the Spirit. That they therefore could be inspired the same as Paul, John, and Peter. We believe Christians are illuminated to the knowledge of Scriptural truth. This is much different than inspiration. There are times, for the writers of Scripture, when the Holy Ghost inspired their words, but did not grant the knowledge of the meaning of the words.

The Dictation Theory

P. B. Fitzwater states in *Christian Theology:* "This theory makes the writers of the Scriptures passive in the hand of the Holy Spirit. It holds that the writers were mere machines; therefore, there was no room left for the expression of the individuality of the writer — there was no room for variety of style. This theory stands self-condemned, because the literary critic knows quite well that there is a definite individuality expressed in the writings of various authors."

The Thought or Concept Theory

The thoughts or concepts were given by God, and that the writers by the natural powers actually expressed the thought. This is unacceptable, as words express thought. A study of the Bible shows that a word may be important or even crucial (Matthew 12:37; John 10:35; Galatians 3:16).

Every word is Divinely inspired. We believe the Scriptures to be perfectly planned. Not a word too little nor too much, and that the authors (as Bishop Hooker puts it) "Neither spoke nor wrote one word of their own, but uttered syllable by syllable as the Spirit put it into their mouths."

The Plenary-Verbal Theory

The Plenary-verbal inspiration of Scripture is that which we believe. The word Plenary means "full," "complete" in every respect, and verbal "word," means that every word of Scripture is inspired. The Law, the Prophets, the Gospels, the Epistles, and the Revelation. These are not partially inspired as some would have us believe. They are complete; the Bible is the Word of God.

SCRIPTURAL PROOF OF INSPIRATION

The proof of inspiration of Scripture gives the Christian faith a sure foundation. Every believer ought to be able to give a reason for his hope, ", . . be ready always to give an answer to every man that asketh you a reason of the hope that is in you" (1 Peter 3:15).

The Scripture speaks for itself in proof of inspiration. "All scripture is given by inspiration of God, and is profitable for doctrine, for reproof, for correction, for instruction in righteousness" (2 Timothy 3:16). "For the prophecy came not in old time by the will of man: but holy men of God spake as they were moved by the Holy Ghost" (2 Peter 1:21).

Throughout the Bible there are statements as, "the word of God," "the word of the Lord," and "my word." The term "and God said," or its equivalent, is used over 2,600 times. Jesus accepted the Old Testament as the infallible Word of God. "For verily I say unto you, Till heaven and earth pass, one jot or one tittle shall in no wise pass from the law, till all be fulfilled" (Matthew 5:18). He endorsed its truth and authority (Matthew 5:18; John 10:35; Luke 18:31-33). The apostles speak with Divine authority (1 Corinthians 2:13; 14:31; 1 Thessalonians 2:13; 4:2; 2 Peter 3:2; 1 John 1:5; Revelation 1:1).

The Development of Doctrine

No man has the ability in developing the doctrine of God, salvation, or immortality. A good example of this development is given by J. McKee Adams in *Our Bible:*

"The progressive unfolding of the divine plan and purpose to save is recounted through all the pages of the Old Testament from the earliest days to the latest. Patriarchs, lawgivers, priests, prophets, and teachers make mention of the purpose of God as revealed both to individuals and the nation. The great figure on whom this development centers is the Messiah. His mission in the world is solely for salvation. The whole history of the Hebrew people, from the time of Abraham to the advent of Jesus, is unified in the person and mission of the Messiah. God promised Abraham in Ur of the Chaldees that in him and his seed the nations of the earth would be blessed. That promise was fulfilled with the coming of Jesus in Bethlehem of Judea two thousand years later."

Fulfillment of Prophecy

Fulfillment of prophecy is certainly proof of Divine inspiration. "Remember the former things of old: for I am God, and there is none else; I am God, and there is none like me, Declaring the end from the beginning, and from ancient times the things that are not yet done, saying, My counsel shall stand, and I will do all my pleasure" (Isaiah 46:9, 10).

"No one but Almighty God, who knows the end from the beginning, could reveal what is so minutely foretold by the prophets concerning individuals, cities, nations and the world, but most minutely of all concerning the birth, ministry, message, death, and resurrection of Christ and His coming glory" (1 Peter 1:10, 11).

The Unity of Scripture

Authors of the Scripture were from various walks of life. They included priests, kings, statesmen, and shepherds. The Bible contains different types of writings: poetry, prose, history, and prophecy. With all these differences there is a marvelous unity from the beginning to the end. This makes the study of the Scriptures interesting as well as profitable.

The Bible was written by about 40 men who engaged in writing it during a period of about 1600 years dating from 1500 B.C. to about 100 years after Christ. It consists of 39 books in the Old Testament and 27 books in the New Testament. These men wrote as they were moved by the Holy Spirit (2 Peter 1:21). They wrote not in words of human wisdom but in words taught by the Holy Ghost (1 Corinthians 2:13)

SUMMARY

We believe that all the Scripture is inspired — that God used men without taking away their personalities in their writings. This is another one of God's great miracles.

We believe that the Bible speaks for itself, that its author is God. Having accepted the Scriptures as Plenary-verbally inspired, the theories of man should be rejected. We believe the claim of the Bible has been verified in the experiences of millions in all ages. The Bible has worked. It has influenced civilization, transformed lives, brought light, inspiration and comfort to millions. And its work continues.

In this day when modernists and liberals try to discredit the Bible and its Author, let us re-affirm our belief in the "Holy Bible" and its teaching that God is, " ... and that He is a rewarder of them that diligently seek him" (Hebrews 11:6). With faith in the infallible Word of God you shall, " ... be ready always to give an answer to every man that asketh you a reason of the hope that is in you" (1 Peter 3:15).

DISCUSSION QUESTIONS

1. What do we mean when we say: "We believe that the Bible is the inspired word of God?"
2. Is every word inspired?
3. What is Plenary-verbal inspiration?
4. What Biblical proof is there for inspiration of Scripture?

5. What is the difference between revelation and inspiration?
6. How would you define inspiration?
7. Give some modern theories of inspiration.
8. Do you believe there are degrees of inspiration?
9. Discuss the unity of the Bible.
10. Has archaeology had any effect on the Bible?

BOOKS RECOMMENDED FOR STUDY

Adams, J. McKee, *Our Bible.* Nashville: Convention Press, 1937.

Brewster, P. S., *Pentecostal Doctrine.* Gloucestershire, England: P. S. Brewster, 1976.

Fitzwater, P. B., *Christian Theology.* Grand Rapids: William B. Eerdmans, 1948.

Geisler, Norman L. and William E. Nix. *A General Introduction to the Bible.* Chicago: Moody Press, 1968.

Nelson, P. C., *Bible Doctrines.* Springfield: Gospel Publishing House, 1971.

Pearlman, Myer, *Knowing The Doctrines Of The Bible.* Springfield: Gospel Publishing House, 1937.

CHAPTER 2

THE TRINITY

Our God is a trinity in unity, manifested in three persons: the Father, the Son, and the Holy Spirit. God is infinitely perfect, being in His three persons co-existent, co-equal, and co-eternal.

God the Father is greater than all (John 14:28); the source of the Word (LOGOS) and the Begetter (John 16:28; John 1:14).

The Son was the begotten of the Father, accepting earthly limitations, true God and true man; conceived by the Holy Ghost and born of the Virgin Mary. He died upon the cross, the Just for the unjust as a substitutionary sacrifice, and all who believe in Him are justified on the grounds of His shed blood. He arose from the dead according to the Scriptures. He is now at the right hand of the Majesty on High as our great High Priest, and He will return again to establish His Kingdom of righteousness and justice.

The Holy Spirit is a Divine Person, Executive of the Godhead on earth, the Comforter sent by the Lord Jesus Christ to indwell, to guide, and to teach the believer and to convince the world of sin, of righteousness, and of judgment.

In this lesson the objective will be to show the Scriptural teaching of the three personalities of God. It is not my intention to deal with each one in His distinctive office work. As a student of God's word, a study of the personality of God the Father, the personality of God the Son, and the personality of the Holy Ghost, as well as the attributes of God would be most profitable to a greater understanding of the Trinity.

The term Trinity is not used in the Bible. But, the doctrine of the Trinity is taught throughout the Scriptures — a subject too vast for the finite mind to comprehend. As Herbert Lockyer puts it, "Truly, our narrow thoughts can no more comprehend the Trinity in Unity than a nutshell can hold all the water in the sea!" Yet, we must accept the teaching of Scripture.

The Trinity of God

The idea of the term "Trinity" is three in one. This mysterious doctrine is beyond the comprehension of finite mind, and must be received as true on the authority of the Bible.

I have found no better definition of the term Trinity than is given by Webster's Dictionary, "The union of three persons (the Father, the Son, and the Holy Spirit) in one Godhead, so that all the three are one God as to substance, but three persons as to individuality."

Divine Unity

In the Trinity there is a compound unity. Three distinct persons, with each person being supremely conscious of the other two. Unity applies to God's essence. Trinity applies to His personality. It has been said, "We cannot by any amount of searching find out God." The more we try, the more we are bewildered. It is only through Jesus Christ we are to see God. He came to reveal God's love to man. Brumback states in *God in Three Persons:*

"In a true sense God is one, and in an equally true sense the three members of the Godhead are distinct. It is both reasonable and scriptural to say that there is one divine essence or nature which all have in common, and yet, there are three mutually related and distinct centers of consciousness, knowledge, love and will."

Each person in the Godhead has his own distinct office of operation, yet they always act in unison. The Scriptures teach that every plan and purpose of the Godhead is carried out jointly by the Father, the Son, and the Holy Ghost. As an example, the Father originated and devised the plan of salvation, the Son came to earth and executed the plan, and the Holy Ghost applies salvation to each individual who believes.

Without Analogy

The Trinity transcends human powers of thought, and there is no analogy to it on earth. The human personality in its triune nature is the nearest approach to a comparison.

But it should be noted that each Person of the Trinity is not part of God; all of the Persons are God, complete in themselves in their respective spheres, yet they are but one God.

The Trinity could be further illustrated as the universe is presented to us as earth, sea and sky. Atmosphere is made of light, heat and air. Matter itself is solids, liquids, and gases. Water is ice, liquid and vapor. From the sun we have light, heat and chemical effects. These are good illustrations, but in the real sense the doctrine of the Trinity is a mystery, which defies the comprehension of every finite mind, and must be received as true on the authority of the Bible. I confess myself unable to adequately explain this mystery. I receive the FACT of this great doctrine, simply because I believe that the Scriptures reveal the FACT.

SCRIPTURAL PROOF OF THREE PERSONS

The Plural Name for God

Elohim is a plural form of the Hebrew word for God. The name "Elohim" is the name God gave Himself in the beginning of the Bible. It is used by Moses hundreds of times in referring to God in the Old Testament, and is used more frequently in the New Testament. This mountain of proof of the Trinity cannot be explored in one short lesson, therefore the following are a few of these Scriptural references.

Plural Pronouns

Let us consider a few Scriptures that use the plural pronoun. "And God said, Let us make man in our image, after our likeness ... (Genesis 1:26). "And the Lord God said, Behold, the man is become as one of us . . ." (Genesis 3:22). "Go to, let us go down, and there confound their languages . . ." (Genesis 11:7)... "Whom shall I send, and who will go for us?" (Isaiah 6:8).

Personal Pronouns

The argument in favor of the doctrine of the Trinity supplied by the use of the personal pronouns, "I, Thou, He," is worthy of some expansion. The passages in the Bible are almost numberless in which God, in referring to Himself, says, I, mine, and me: "As I live, saith the Lord;" "I am the Lord;" "All souls are mine;" "Every beast of the forest is mine;" "Besides me there is no Saviour;" "Prove me now herewith, saith the Lord of hosts." There are passages, too, in which the Father and the Son say to each other thou, thee, and thine: "Thou art my Son; this day have I begotten thee;" "Thou hast loved righteousness;" "As thou hast given him power over all flesh;" "All mine are thine, and thine are mine." While the Father and the Son address each other in the use of the personal pronouns, thou, thee, and thine, the Spirit is referred to as he and him: "But the comforter, which is the Holy Ghost, whom the Father will send in my name, he shall teach you all things" (John 14:26); "He shall glorify me" (16:14); "The Comforter whom I will send unto you" (15:26). It is needless to multiply proofs that the Spirit was to be sent by the Father and the Son. The Father is said to have sent the Son into the world, but neither the Son nor the Spirit is ever said to have sent the Father. The Son is represented as becoming flesh and dying, but this is not true of the Father and the Spirit. In view of these significant facts it is obvious that there is such a threefold distinction of persons in the Godhead as to justify and to require the use of the terms Father, Son, and Spirit. Nor does this threefold distinction conflict with the unity of God, for the three persons are one in substance, while they are three in individuality. These two truths present unity in Trinity. (James M. Pendleton)

Conversation of the Persons of the Godhead

Here we consider a few Scriptures where there is conversation between persons of the Godhead. "Then said he, Lo, I come to do thy will, O God . . ." (Hebrews 10:9). "Wherefore when he cometh into the world, he saith, Sacrifice and offering thou wouldest not, but a body hast thou prepared me" (Hebrews 10:5). "Father, glorify thy name. Then came there a voice from heaven, saying, I have both glorified it, and will glorify it again" (John 12:28). "For thou wilt not leave my soul in hell; neither wilt thou suffer thine Holy One to see corruption" (Psalm 16:10). "... the Lord hath said unto me, Thou art my Son; this day have I begotten thee" (Psalm 2:7). "Thy throne, O God, is for ever and ever . . ." (Psalm 45:6). "The Lord said unto my Lord, Sit thou at my right hand, until I make thine enemies thy footstool" (Psalm 110:1).

Three Personalities are Recognized as God

In the mouth of two or three witnesses let every word be established. (1) The Father as God: ". . . for him hath God the Father sealed" (John 6:27). "Elect according to the foreknowledge of God the Father . . ." (1 Peter 1:2). (2) The Son as God: ".. . the Word was God (John 1:1). "But unto the Son he saith, Thy throne, 0 God..." (Hebrews 1:8). (3) The Holy Ghost as God: " ... to lie to the Holy Ghost... thou hast... lied . . . unto God" (Acts 5:3-4). " . . . the temple of the Holy Ghost" . . . "the temple of God" (1 Corinthians 6:19; 3:16).

More Than One Referred to in the Epistles

Many places refer to more than one in the Scriptures. The following are some examples from the Epistles. "... Grace to you and peace from God our Father, and the Lord Jesus Christ" (Romans 1:7). "Grace be unto you, and peace, from God our Father, and from the Lord Jesus Christ" (1 Corinthians 1:3). Other examples: 2 Corinthians 1:2; Galatians 1:3; Ephesians 1:2; Philippians 1:2; Colossians 1:2; 1 Thessalonians 1:1; 2 Thessalonians 1:2; 1 Timothy 1:2; 2 Timothy 1:2; Titus 1:4; Philemon 1:3; James 1:1; 1 Peter 1:2; 2 Peter 1:2; 2 John 3.

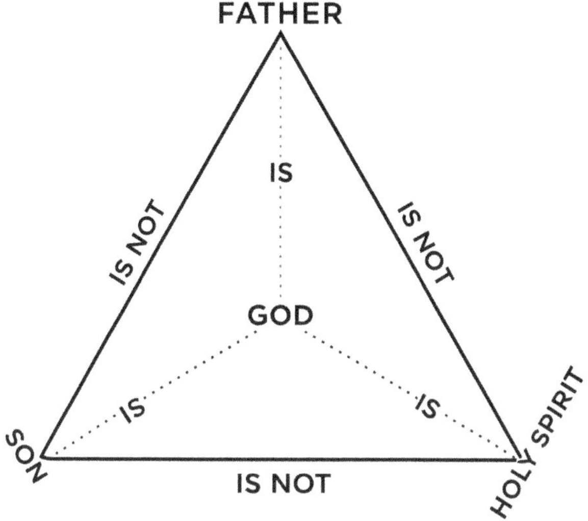

An Erroneous Doctrinal View

In the early days of the Pentecostal movement, there was a small segment of preachers that promoted the "Oneness" or "Jesus Only" doctrine. There are some groups in the Pentecostal movement today who believe in the "Jesus Only" doctrine. We believe an overwhelming majority have experienced the new birth and the baptism of the Spirit. It is not our thought then to judge their experience, but, rather to address our remarks to the doctrine.

Those who believe in Jesus only — that Jesus alone is God — must believe the following statements: That Jesus is His own father (Acts 13:33). That He begot Himself (John 3:16). That He prayed to Himself and thanked Himself (John 11:41-42; 14:28). That He anointed Himself with Himself and accompanied Himself on earth (Acts 10:38). That He prayed to Himself to forgive those who crucified Him (Luke 23:24). That He forsook Himself on the cross (Matthew 27:46). That He is sitting on His own right hand (Hebrews 1:3).

For an in-depth study of a Trinitarian answer to the Oneness or "Jesus Only" doctrine, I would recommend: *God in Three Persons*, by Carl Brumback.

SUMMARY

We believe the doctrine of the Trinity to be an indisputable fact as taught in Scripture — that it cannot be eliminated from the precious Word of God. We believe that it is a mystery so profound that the wisest of earth have had to confess their inability to understand it.

We believe the Father to be the source of the Word, the Begetter of the Son (John 16:28).

We believe the Son was begotten of the Father, conceived by the Holy Ghost, and was born of the Virgin Mary.

We believe the Holy Spirit is a Divine person, and is the executive of the Godhead on earth.

The three persons in one Godhead cannot be fully comprehended by the finite mind, but must be accepted on grounds of vast Biblical truth.

We believe all the characteristics and attributes of God are applied equally to all the persons of the Trinity. They are coeternal, omniscient, omnipotent and omnipresent.

Praise God, from whom all blessings flow;

Praise Him, all creatures here below;

Praise Him above, ye heavenly host;

Praise FATHER, SON, AND HOLY GHOST.

DISCUSSION QUESTIONS

1. How many Gods are there?
2. What does the term Triune mean?
3. How can three persons be one God?
4. What are some of the compound names for God?
5. How would you respond to the "Oneness" doctrine?
6. Name the three personalities of God.
7. Are the conversations of the persons of the Godhead clear?
8. Are the three persons of the Godhead co-existent, coequal, and co-eternal?
9. Is the Holy Ghost a person?
10. Is God perfect?

BOOKS RECOMMENDED FOR STUDY

Brewster, P. S. *Pentecostal Doctrine.* Gloucestershire, England: P. S. Brewster, 1976.

Brumback, Carl. *God In Three Persons.* Cleveland: Pathway Press, 1959.

Lockyer. Herbert. *All The Doctrines Of The Bible.* Grand Rapids: ZonderSvan Publishing House, 1977.

Nelson, P. C. *Bible Doctrines.* Springfield: Gospel Publishing House, 1971.

Pendleton, James M. *Christian Doctrines.* Philadelphia: The Judson Press, 1960.

CHAPTER 3
MAN, HIS FALL AND REDEMPTION

Man is a created being, made in the likeness and the image of God, but through Adam's transgressions and fall, sin came into the world (Romans 5:12). "All have sinned and come short of the glory of God" (Romans 3:23). "As it is written, there is none righteous, no not one" (Romans 3:10). Jesus Christ, the Son of God, was manifested to undo the work of the devil and gave His life and shed His blood to redeem and restore man back to God (1 John 3:8).

Salvation is the gift of God to man, separate from works and the Law, and is made operative by grace through faith in Jesus Christ, producing works acceptable to God (Ephesians 2:8).

The subject "Man, His Fall and Redemption," is too large to adequately cover in one lesson. Our concern is to give some Biblical facts about the doctrine of man, facts about man's origin, what happened in the fall, and how man is redeemed. When referring to man: the simple meaning, a human being, male or female is used. It is not our purpose to go fully into the doctrine of anthropology, but rather to give the student a foundation on which to build.

THE ORIGIN OF MAN

Theory of Man's Origin

The origin of man is something he, himself has tried to figure out. When he tries, his theory has missing links. He says, "If only I could find the missing link." Of the many theories on evolution, Darwin's theory is accredited to be the best. But, it is only a theory, without fact. Many distinguished scientists declare that Darwin's theory has been discarded, because it has not been verified.

Scientists have now been at work for many years in exploring lands and seas, in examining the fossil remains of countless species of plants and animals, and in applying all the inventive genius of man to obtain and perpetuate new varieties and races, they have never yet been able to exhibit a single decisive proof that a transformation of species has

ever taken place. Animals are now as they were represented on the pyramids or found mummified in the tombs of Egypt, as they were before they left their fossil forms in the rocks. Many species have become extinct, others are found of which no very ancient specimens have been discovered; but it cannot be proved that any species ever evolved from another.

The Bible only gives us the facts about man's origin: "And God said, Let us make man in our image, after our likeness: and let them have dominion over the fish of the sea, and over the fowl of the air, and over the cattle, and over all the earth, and over every creeping thing that creepeth upon the earth. So God created man in his own image, in the image of God created he him; male and female created he them" (Genesis 1:27).

We totally reject the theory of evolution as to man's origin. There is no concrete evidence to support that man originally was a protoplasm, and that he evolved into an ape, and then in some myste-rious way became a man. Myer Pearlman in *Knowing the Doctrines of the Bible,* gives an example of the futile attempts of the evolu-tionists:

"Evolutionists have imagined a type of creature through which the ape passed into the human stage. This is the "missing link," which has been named Pithecanthropus Erectus. Evidence: Some years ago a few bones — two teeth one thigh bone and a part of a skull cap — were discovered on the island of Java. With the addition of plaster of Paris they reconstructed the link which connects man with the lower creation! Other 'links' have been constructed in similar fashion. But Dr. Etheridge, examiner of the British Museum, said, in all this great museum there is not a particle of evidence of the transmutation of species. This museum is full of proofs of the utter falsity of these views.' "

Creation, Man's Origin

The origin of man is the result of Divine counsel. There was a counsel in eternity in which the decree was made to bring man into existence. In the early chapters of Genesis and elsewhere in the Bible, the creation of man is clearly taught. "The Holy Scriptures must ever be our authority concerning the origin of mankind. Two accounts are recorded in Genesis. The first is brief, and is found in connection with the account of the animal creation on the sixth day (Genesis 1:26-30); the second is more extended and stands by itself (Genesis 2:4-25). There is no discrepancy in the accounts. Brief as they may be, we have here the only authoritative account of man's origin. The new order of being involved, and its pre-eminence over the animal creation are indicated by a change in the form of the creative fiat. No longer do we have the words, "Let there be," which involve the immediacy of the creative fiat in conjunction with secondary causes; but "Let us make man in our image, after our likeness" — an expression which asserts the power of the creative word in conjunction with deliberative counsel." (Chafer, page 165)

Man's origin was an act of the Triune God, as given in the inspired Scriptures. "And God said, Let us make man in our image, after our likeness: and let them have dominion over the fish of the sea, over the fowl of the air, and over the cattle, and over all the earth, and over every creeping thing that creepeth upon the earth" (Genesis 1:26).

Man was Created in the Image of God

Man was created in the image and likeness of God, good and upright, and endowed with intelligence, conscience and will, so that he could hold dominion over all living things on earth and exercise free choice (Genesis 1:26; Psalm 8:4-8).

Man was created God-like; he was made like God in character and personality. Man was made in God's image, a rational, intellectual being. ". . . made after the similitude of God" (James 3:9).

Man was made in the moral image of God. He was created a holy being. Our first parents came from the hand of God, as spotless as the angels in heaven. His disposition was right. His heart was right. His joy was complete. Every desire was gratified, every want was supplied. What a beautiful state!

THE FALL OF MAN

The fall of man was from the perfect state in which God had created him. We do not know how long man lived in this perfect state. In this perfect state it should have been easy for man to remain perfect. Surely God intended for it to be easy for man to continue in this perfect state. God placed only one prohibition on man, "But of the tree of knowledge of good and evil, thou shalt not eat of it: for in the day that thou eatest thereof thou shalt surely die" (Genesis 2:17).

The Introduction of Sin

Satan appeared in the form of a serpent, a creature which at that time was very beautiful and attractive. "Now the serpent was more subtle than any beast of the field which the Lord God had made. And he said unto the woman, Yea, hath God said, Ye shall not eat of every tree of the garden?" (Genesis 3:1).

Satan is referred to as the tempter. He tempts Eve to doubt God. Temptation is not sin, the yielding to temptation is sin. As stated in the *Pulpit Commentary:* "The first temptation is the type of all temptation. Notice the three points: — (1) falsification of fact and confusion of mind; (2) alienation from God as the Source of all good and the only wise Ruler of our life; (3) desire selfishly exalting itself above the recognized and appointed limits."

The method Satan used is the same he uses today. He found the woman while she was alone. He insinuated doubt into Eve's mind. Satan raised a question as to God's word and God's love.

Man's Disobedience

The steps in man's fall seem to have been rapid. From doubting God's word, to doubting His love. From desiring (lusting after) what God had prohibited, to indulgence. Sin is not a necessary fault of man because of defective material or some maladjustment. Man's sin was a free action. Adam's act was not a casual slip, but deliberate disobedience. Adam's transgression and fall has brought sin into the world. "Wherefore, as by one man sin entered into the world, and death by sin; and so death passed upon all men, for that all have sinned" (Romans 5:12).

The Consequences of Man's Disobedience

When Adam and Eve sinned they lost their blessed estate in which both had been created, and they became subject to certain far-reaching changes. God had said, ". . . for in the day that thou eatest thereof thou shalt surely die" (Genesis 2:17).

Also the following are some of the consequences of man's fall: (a) Enmity between the seed of the woman and the seed of the serpent, the cause of wars and bloodshed (Genesis 3:15). (b) The judgment upon the woman (Genesis 3:16). (c) Earth cursed (Genesis 3:17, 18). (d) Death (Genesis 3:19). (e) Expulsion from the garden (Genesis 3:24).

Those consequences have befallen the whole human race. "Therefore as by the offense of one judgment came upon all men to condemnation; even so by the righteousness of one the free gift came upon all men unto justification of life. For as by one man's disobedience many were made sinners, so by the obedience of one shall many be made righteous" (Romans 5:19, 20).

REDEMPTION

What it Means to be Redeemed

The word "redeem" in both Old and New Testament means to buy back by the paying of a price; to loose from bondage by the paying of a price; to buy in a market and to take from a market. The Lord Jesus is a Redeemer and His atoning work is described as a redemption. Matthew 20:28; Revelation 5:9; 14:3, 4; Galatians 3:13; 4:5; Titus 2:14; 1 Peter 1:18.

There is a good illustration given of redemption in Leviticus 25:47-49. (1) Here the redeemer was to be kin to the one to be redeemed.

(2) He must be willing to redeem or buy back. (3) He must have the price.

Christ became kin to us by taking our nature. He was willing to give up all to redeem us. He was able to pay the price — His own precious blood.

The Price of Redemption

It cost something to redeem fallen man. The Son of Man came into the world "… to give his life a ransom [or redemption] for many" (Matthew 20:28). The most wonderful verse in all Scripture of the price of redemption is, "For God so loved the world, that he gave his only begotten son, that whosoever believeth in him should not perish, but have everlasting life" (John 3:16). In God's plan of redemption, He himself provided the price. Such a great price — a gift from God, that all the world might be saved. Everyone who believes on Christ can be redeemed. "In whom we have redemption through his blood, the forgiveness of sins, according to the riches of his grace" (Ephesians 1:7).

SUMMARY

Man's creation is an indisputable fact of Scripture. He was created in the image of God. His origin is the result of Divine counsel. Man was created perfect and remained so until the fall. He enjoyed fellowship with God and it is God's desire to restore fallen man to fellowship with him. "God is a spirit; and they that worship him must worship him in spirit and truth" (John 4:24).

Man through transgression fell from the perfect state in which God had created him. Adam's sin was a free act. This transgression of Adam brought sin into the world. "Wherefore, as by one man sin entered into the world, and death by sin; and so death passed upon all men, for that all have sinned" (Romans 5:12).

Through redemption, man has been restored to a state of: (a) Fellowship with God. (b) Now his heart is right with God. (c) He has fullness of joy. (d) He has ". . . the peace of God, which passeth all understanding . . ." (Philippians 4:7).

The cost of this wonderful redemption that we enjoy was great. It cost our Redeemer His life. "How much more shall the blood of Christ, who through the eternal Spirit offered himself without spot to God . . (Hebrews 9:14), obtain our redemption. John says, that "the blood of Jesus Christ his Son cleanseth us from all sin" (1 John 1:7). He paid the price for redemption. When we accepted Him, Satan's power was broken. We now can lead a new life, a holy life, a free life, and a life without any fear, all because of His redeeming love.

DISCUSSION QUESTIONS

1. Do you believe the Scriptural teaching of man's origin?
2. What is the theory of evolution?
3. How is man made in the image of God?
4. What was the state of man before he sinned?
5. How did Satan lie to Eve?
6. What happened when Adam and Eve sinned?
7. Does all creation suffer from Adam's sin?
8. What is man's hope in his fallen state?
9. Did God promise a Redeemer?
10. Is the blood of Christ the only sacrifice for sin?

BOOKS RECOMMENDED FOR STUDY

Fitzwater, P. B. *Christian Theology*. Grand Rapids: William B. Eerdmans, 1948.

Lockyer, Herbert. *All The Doctrines Of The Bible.* Grand Rapids: Zondervan Publishing House, 1977.

Nelson, P. C. *Bible Doctrines.* Springfield: Gospel Publishing House, 1971.

Pearlman, Myer. *Knowing The Doctrines Of The Bible.* Springfield: Gospel Publishing House, 1937.

Wiley, Orton H. *Christian Theology.* II, Kansas City, Mo: Beacon Hill Press, 1952.

CHAPTER 4
THE CHURCH

The true Church is the Body of Jesus Christ (Colossians 1:18; Ephesians 4:15), He being the Head. Its earthly constituents are all true believers, born again by the Spirit (John 3:6) and by the Word (1 Peter 1:23).

To it is delegated the various gifts and offices of the Holy Spirit (1 Corinthians 12:7-11 and 27, 28) necessary for the successful fulfillment of Christ's Great Commission to the Church, as given to the disciples in Matthew 28:19 and Mark 16:15-20.

The doctrine of the Church is one of great importance. Because of the many differences in which the term Church is used, there are such references to the Church as: the Catholic Church, the Protestant Church, the Liberal Church, the Conservative Church, the Modern Church, the Evangelical Church, the Fundamental Church, and the Pentecostal Church. To these many more could be added, but these are some of the commonly used terms. In each of these groups there are many different denominations and churches. Ignorance concerning the Church is the real secret of man's indifference toward it. Many of the abuses of the Church can be traced likewise to man's failure to understand its essential nature. Those who have come to know its real meaning prize highly the privilege of membership in it and have a definite passion to enlist others as members thereof.

USAGES OF THE TERM "CHURCH"

An Assembly

This term "assembly" is a place where people meet. This does not always mean that those gathered together constitute a New Testament church. This assembling together may not have anything to do with being a Christian. As Christians, we are to follow the teaching of Scripture, to assemble together. "Not forsaking the assembling of ourselves together, as the manner of some is; but exhorting one another: and so much the more, as ye see the day approaching" (Hebrews 10:25).

A Local Assembly of Believers

The apostle Paul was referring to local assemblies when it is said, "And he went through Syria and Cilicia, confirming the churches" (Acts 15:41). Also the local assemblies were referred to as the churches of the Gentiles (Romans 16: 4). Again, Paul said, ". . . the grace of God bestowed on the churches of Macedonia" (2 Corinthians 8:1), referring to assemblies of local believers.

A Body of Professing Believers

The word "church" in this sense embraces all church members — all who have made a profession of faith in Jesus Christ. This is usually known as the "visible Church." "Now about that time Herod the king stretched forth his hands to vex certain of the church" (Acts 12:1). "For ye have heard of my conversation in time past in the Jews' religion, how that beyond measure I persecuted the church of God, and wasted it" (Galatians 1:13). Here Paul speaks of a time when he persecuted the true Church, thinking he was doing God a favor. There are those professing to be believers today, who, it seems, give little thought of speaking harmfully about another member of the body of Christ. These who profess, and have not had an experience with Christ, can be found in most any body of professing believers. Only God knows those who are really members of the body of Christ.

THE BODY OF CHRIST

The Invisible Church

The New Testament uses the word "church" some 114 times. 111 references are to the body of Christ. Paul says, "Now ye are the body of Christ, and members in particular" (1 Corinthians 12:27).

Romanism thinks of the Church as an external and visible organization only. We, as Pentecostal believers, hold that the Church of Jesus Christ is an invisible and spiritual communion of saints, and He is the head. "And hath put all things under his feet, and gave him to be the head over all things to the church" (Ephesians 1:22).

The Scriptures speak of His ownership of the Church. "Unto the church of God which is at Corinth, to them that are sanctified in Christ Jesus, called to be saints, with all that in every place call upon the name of Jesus Christ our Lord, both their's and our's" (1 Corinthians 1:2). "But if I tarry long, that thou mayest know how thou oughtest to behave thyself in the house of God, which is the church of the living God, the pillar and ground of the truth" (1 Timothy 3:15). "To the general assembly and church of the firstborn, which are written in heaven, and to God the Judge of all, and to the spirits of just men made perfect" (Hebrews 12:23). The term "church" comes from the Greek word "Ecclesia" which means "to call out from among." The Church is a body of people called out from the world, redeemed by His blood. His love for His Church is shown in, "Husbands, love your wives, even as Christ also loved the church, and gave himself for it" (Ephesians 5:25).

The Church is a Unique Body

The Church of Jesus Christ is an *organized* organism. An organism is a whole made up of related parts that work together. "For as the body is one, and hath many members, and all the members of that one body, being many, are one body: so also is Christ" (1 Corinthians 12:12). "But now hath God set the members every one of them in the body, as it hath pleased him" (1 Corinthians 12:18). "Now ye are the body of Christ, and members in particular. And God hath set some in the church, first apostles, secondarily prophets, thirdly teachers, after that miracles, then gifts of healings, helps, governments, diversities of tongues" (1 Corinthians 12:27, 28).\

Entrance Into the Body

It is possible to belong to a church without being a member of the Church of Jesus Christ. Only those who have been born again are members of His Church. " . . . And the Lord added to the church daily such as should be saved" (Acts 2:47)."Many think that the Church is a voluntary, social institution for the mutual strengthening of its members, forgetting that regeneration is the absolute requirement for entrance therein and that all regenerated persons in this dispensation are baptized into that one body by the sovereign act of the Holy Spirit. Failure to see this reveals the tragic blunder of persuading unregenerate people to enter the church to obtain salvation and enjoy its social benefits. Only the regenerate can possibly be members of Christ's body, the church. It is blessedly true that saved people enjoy great social benefits and personal pleasure. The fellowship of the redeemed is a high privilege both in this life and the life to come. Therefore, the Church is a unique body. It is unlike all earthly associations which are founded upon natural similarities or complements such as taste, wealth, culture, nationality, or dignity of birth, or upon the oldest and most fundamental of all earthly relations, the basis of sex. In the Church, however, age, wealth, culture, birth, nationality, and sex are not recognized. In Christ Jesus 'There is neither Jew nor Greek, there is neither bond nor free, there is neither male nor female: for ye are all one in Christ Jesus' (Galatians 3:28)." *(Fitzwater*, Page 468).

This unique body has been called out by God, and selected for a particular purpose. That purpose: to do a work for Him in bringing others into the Church. He seeks a Church "That he might present it to himself a glorious church, not having spot, or wrinkle, or any such thing; but that it should be holy and without blemish" (Ephesians 5:27).

Those who enter this body will do so by "Being born again, not of corruptible seed, but of incorruptible, by the word of God, which liveth and abideth for ever." (1 Peter 1:23). We are further told, "And there shall in no wise enter into it any thing that defileth, neither whatsoever worketh abomination, or maketh a lie: but they which are written in the Lamb's book of life." (Revelation 21:27).

THE FUNCTION OF THE CHURCH

The Church is to Teach and Preach

The Church is a Divine institution, designed by God to be more than just a building. But God does not really dwell in material buildings as such (Acts 7:48, 49; 17:24, 25). His special presence is manifested today in a spiritual temple — the Church. Each believer is a temple of the Holy Spirit (1 Corinthians 6:19), but the entire Church is also described as the temple of God (1 Corinthians 3:16,17; 2 Corinthians 6:16-18). Christ is the chief cornerstone of this spiritual temple, the apostles and prophets are the foundation (Ephesians 2:20-22) and each believer is a "living stone" in the edifice (1 Peter 2:5). As a counterpart of the Old Testament Tabernacle and Temple, this spiritual building is a place where God is worshiped and served. (Nelson, p. 106)

The Lord equipped the Church with offices and gifts. "And he gave some, apostles; and some, prophets; and some, evangelists; and some, pastors and teachers; For the perfecting of the saints, for the work of the ministry, for the edifying of the body of Christ" (Ephesians 4:11-12).

This job of teaching and preaching is given as a command to the Church. "Go ye therefore, and teach all nations, baptizing them in the name of the Father, and of the Son, and of the Holy Ghost. Teaching them to observe all things whatsoever I have commanded you: and, lo, I am with you always, even unto the end of the world" (Matthew 28:19, 20).

The early Church felt, and rightly so, that they were called out to do a job. This is the purpose of the Church of Jesus Christ today, to do the job of evangelism. In order to carry out the great commission, every local church ought to have in operation the ministries of: Evangelists, pastors and teachers, helps, governments, administrations, the gifts of the Spirit, and the fruit of the Spirit. The Church was visibly established on the day of Pentecost, through the operation of the Holy Spirit. Soon after, we see these gifts manifested in the Church. We Pentecostals know the joy of having the Holy Spirit move in our local services, implementing these special gifts.

Paul, writing to the Corinthians, says there are diversities of gifts as well as the operation of the gifts. "But the manifestation of the Spirit is given to every man to profit withal. For to one is given by the Spirit the word of wisdom; to another the word of knowledge by the same Spirit; To another faith by the same Spirit; to another the gifts of healing by the same Spirit; To another the working of miracles; to another prophecy; to another, discerning of spirits; to another divers kinds of tongues; to another the interpretation of tongues: But all these worketh that one and the selfsame Spirit, dividing to every man severally as he will. For as the body is one, and hath many members, and all the members of that one body, being many, are one body: so also is Christ" (1 Corinthians 12:7-12).

Love is to Prevail

If our work is to be done effectively, love must prevail. Jesus said, "A new commandment I give unto you, That ye love one another" (John 13:34). This love is to be without hypocrisy. "Be kindly affectioned one to another with brotherly love; in honor preferring one another" (Romans 12:10).

The Unity of the Church

Every Bible reference speaks of unity. The Church is called the bride, the body, and a building. The Church is the temple of the living God, and its people are said to be a royal priesthood, a peculiar people, a holy nation. Brewster says in *Pentecostal Doctrine:* "This unity does not mean for a moment that our traditions are always the same. There is not uniformity in the Church, but there is a blessed unity. It is not even the total unanimity of doctrine. There are minor points about which we do not necessarily agree, but again this does not militate against the unity of the Church, because the unity of the Church is the unity of its relationship, the unity of its relationship to Christ. The difference can be illustrated by contrasting a bag of marbles and a bunch of grapes. On the one hand there is total uniformity but no unity. As to the bunch of grapes, they are all different shapes and sizes, but they have one central stem, and so aptly describe the fundamental unity of the Church. It has the one life from the one source" (p. 141).

Unity produces a healthy state of another vital part of the Church, the "Worship Service." We Pentecostals are known for a very lively service; we worship Him in song, in praise, in prayer, in the preaching and teaching of Biblical truth, and in giving. Yes, we believe giving of our money is an act of worship.

Protection for the Church

The Spirit of truth and error is to be tested, proved and exposed or substantiated by the Church. Many of the problems we encounter in the Church today derive from the lack of protection from false or erroneous teaching. The warning is to "Beware of false prophets, which come to you in sheep's clothing, but inwardly they are ravening wolves" (Matthew 7:15).

The danger is stated again in the book of Acts. This will be covered further in the chapter on "The Ministry." Here let's look at the need for protection. "Take heed therefore unto yourselves, and to all the flock, over the which the Holy Ghost hath made you overseers, to feed the church of God, which he hath purchased with his own blood. For I know this, that after my departing shall grievous wolves enter in among you, not sparing the flock" (Acts 20:28, 29).

Discipline

The Bible example is the one we are to follow; if we follow this example, offenses, disputes and trespasses are settled. Instructions as given in Matthew. "Moreover if thy brother shall trespass against thee, go and tell him his fault between thee and him alone: if he shall hear thee, thou hast gained thy brother. But if he will not hear thee, then take with thee one or two more, that in the mouth of two or three witnesses every word may be established. And if he shall neglect to hear them, tell it unto the church: but if he neglect to hear the church, let him be unto thee as an heathen man and a publican" (Matthew 18:15-17).

We ask our members to subscribe to the following covenant:

> I agree by the grace of God to abide by the rules and/or the constitution and by-laws of this church and to adhere to its doctrines, to attend the means of grace regularly as I have opportunity, and to work in harmony with others of like precious faith for the upbuilding of the kingdom of God for the edifying of the body of Christ and for the advancement of the church.

> I shall endeavor to the best of my ability to walk in the light of God's Word; however, should I change my doctrinal beliefs or cease to live a Godly life, I shall consider it right to be removed from the membership of this church.

We Pentecostals have at times failed in disciplining the offender in the church. The reason given many times is, "I'm afraid they may get offended." A wrongdoer who is allowed to be let go in his own way is not only hurting himself, but others. We have a responsibility to discipline the offending party, that others may be helped.

If members and ministry were to follow wholly the pattern of New Testament truth, the problems of "wishy-washy" members, run-abouts, gab-abouts, church splits, divisions, weak members, and unhealthy state of Church life would be forever solved.

If There Were No Churches

If there were no churches, there would be:
No church fellowship!
No Sunday schools!
No prayer meetings
No Christian homes!
No "salt of the earth"!
No "light of the world"!
No gospel preached to the lost sinners!
No missionaries sent to the foreign fields!
No "body of Christ" in the world!
No rapture and wedding day of the church to look for!
No training courses for the youth of the land!
No family altars!
No preachers to visit the sad and lonely homes!
No prayers for sinners!
No moral training for boys and girls!
No Christian colleges!
No love for the lost sinner!

AUTHOR UNKNOWN

SUMMARY

The doctrine of the Church is the doctrine that every born again believer should be acquainted with. It is by being in the right Church, "the body of Christ," that he can expect to be saved.

The Church of Jesus Christ is a unique body, made up of all born again believers, regardless of denomination or affiliation. We Pentecostals think in terms of our church being a movement. In the early days of this movement the a song was often sung, "I care not what church you may belong to, so long as for Christ you may stand."

The plan of God in this age, through the invisible, sanctified Church, is to witness of Christ's saving grace. All the services of the Church should be such as to attract men and women to Christ. Until the catching away of the Bride, the Church is to be busy carrying out the great commission. "Go ye therefore, and teach all nations, baptizing them in the name of the Father, and of the Son, and of the Holy Ghost: Teaching them to observe all things whatsoever I have commanded you: and, lo, I am with you always, even unto the end of the world" (Matthew 28:19, 20).

DISCUSSION QUESTIONS

1. How many churches are there?
2. What is the difference in organization and organism?
3. What is the Church?
4. Can you join the Church?
5. What is meant by the body of Christ?
6. Do you know what is meant by "Ecclesia"?
7. What are some functions of the church?
8. What is said about Christ's love for the church?
9. Is there a need for discipline in the church?
10. What is the Church to teach and preach?

BOOKS RECOMMENDED FOR STUDY

Brewster, P. S. *Pentecostal Doctrine.* Gloucestershire, England: P. S. Brewster, 1976.

Fitzwater, P. B. *Christian Theology.* Grand Rapids: William B. Eerdmans, 1948.

Lockyer, Herbert. *All The Doctrines Of The Bible.* Grand Rapids: Zondervan Publishing House, 1977.

Nelson, P. C. *Bible Doctrines.* Springfield: Gospel Publishing House, 1971. Pearlman, Myer. *Knowing The Doctrines Of The Bible.* Springfield: Gospel Publishing House, 1937.

CHAPTER 5
THE MINISTRY

God through the Holy Spirit, definitely calls such as He desires to serve as evangelists, pastors and teachers, and specifically endues the ones called with the talents and gifts peculiar to that office or offices (Ephesians 4:11-13). Under no circumstances should anyone be ordained or set apart to any such office unless the calling is distinct and evident.

The minister is a person usually referred to as the preacher. The preacher may hold one or more of the positions mentioned in Ephesians 4:11. In our doctrinal statement in the above paragraph, there are evangelists, pastors and teachers mentioned, with no reference to apostles and prophets. In verse eleven, there are five ministries given, or as some believe, four (pastor-teacher as one). In this study of "the ministry" we are primarily concerned about the ordained minister or the clergy. But there is a broader sense in which every Christian is to be a minister in some way.

THE MINISTER

The Minister's Call

The call into the ministry is a divine call. We believe that this call is distinct and evident. That there is no place in the ministry for anyone who hasn't been called of God. The ordination of ministers is the setting apart of those divinely called to the work of ministering in the church.

Barnabas and Paul were called. "As they ministered to the Lord, and fasted, the Holy Ghost said, Separate me Barnabas and Saul for the work whereunto I have called them" (Acts 13:2). Paul gives thanks to the Lord for his call. "And I thank Christ Jesus our Lord, who hath enabled me, for that he counted me faithful, putting me into the ministry" (1 Timothy 1:12). Fitzwater states: "The minister must have a definite conviction that he is called by God. The part that the church had in the ordination was simply to recognize the Lord's hand in calling the individual and to give recognition to the fact of the Lord's call. The church must have definite assurance of the reality of the divine call before proceeding with the ordination." (p. 481)

Jesus called the twelve personally to follow Him. When Jesus was walking by the Sea of Galilee, He called Peter and Andrew, "And he saith unto them, Follow me, and I will make you fishers of men" (Matthew 4:19). This is just an example of His calling the disciples. Those called were to separate themselves from material endeavors for spiritual service. The Biblical principle is given, "Even so hath the Lord ordained that they which preach the gospel should live of the gospel" (1 Corinthians 9:14).

The Qualifications of the Minister

A list of qualifications as taken from 1 Timothy 3:1-7 and Titus 1:5-10. (1) Above reproach, (2) husband of one wife, (3) temperate, (4) prudent, (5) respectable, (6) hospitable, (7) able to teach, (8) not given to wine, (9) not self-willed, (10) not quick-tempered, (11) not pugnacious, (12) uncontentious, (13) gentle, (14) free from the love of money, (15) one who manages his own house well, (16) a good reputation with those outside the church, (17) love of what is good, (18) just, (19) devout, (20) not a new convert.

In this list of qualifications, Paul is dealing primarily with the minister's reputation, ethics, morality, temperament, habits, and spiritual maturity. So the qualifications for the ministry are more than academic. This does not mean that a man should not work to improve himself. The Scripture says, "Study to shew thyself approved unto God, a workman that needeth not to be ashamed, rightly dividing the word of truth" (2 Timothy 2:15). It is important that a minister know what he believes and why he believes it. If he doesn't know what he believes, he is subject to being swayed by every wind of doctrine.

The Ministering Gift

There is a need today for the operation of all the ministries, not just a part. The Apostles were the "ones sent or commissioned." They were and are our missionaries and pioneers. There is no indication in the New Testament that the office of Apostle has ceased. Much of the world today is unevangelized. Therefore there is a need for the ministry of Apostles today.

The Prophet in the Old Testament was called a seer (1 Samuel 9:9; Isaiah 30:10)." The word 'Prophet" in the New Testament means 'to speak forth for another.' This demands the inspiration of God. It is an office set in the Church so that God can speak to men supernaturally. It is not preaching. The thoughts and language expressed are raised above the ordinary level of the person's natural gift of speech. The Prophet communicates the secrets of the most High. He was formerly called a seer, one who sees supernaturally. The gift of prophecy, as such, does not have this seer characteristic. The Prophet brings the light of divine revelation to bear upon future events. He is not only inspired to forth tell, but also to foretell. 'We have also a more sure word of prophecy whereunto ye do well that ye take heed, as unto a light that shineth in a dark place, until the day dawn and the day star arise in your hearts' (2 Peter 1:19). The ministry is with us to this day." (Brewster, p. 105)

The Evangelists were men like Philip, gifted in soul winning, stirring up cities with word and deed. He is one who announces or proclaims good tidings. These men usually go from place to place. Brewster writes: "The evangelist will be equipped with supernatural evidences. Miracles of healing are the credentials of an evangelist's call. Note in Luke 10:9 that the seventy were commissioned not only to preach, but also to heal the sick. Philip's remarkable ministry in Samaria bore the divine attestation (Acts 8:6). The very best publicity for the kingdom of God is the 'signs and wonders' that the Lord Jesus promised" (p. 108).

Paul gave instructions to Timothy to do the work of an evangelist (2 Timothy 4:5). The pastor-teacher is the overseer and shepherd of God's flock. There have been volumes written on the subject of the pastor. The pastor is an indispensable gift to the church. This ministry is covered in the following section.

The Minister's Responsibility

The Christian minister's work is essentially pastoral — the ministry of a shepherd. Christ is the Chief and Great Shepherd and the pastor is the under-shepherd. "Take heed therefore unto yourselves, and to all the flock, over the which the Holy Ghost hath made you overseers, to feed the church of God, which he hath purchased with his own blood" (Acts 20:28). This warning to shepherds comes because there would be grievous wolves enter in, not sparing the flock of God. The price that was paid for the flock, Christ's shed blood, makes the shepherd to feel very keenly the responsibility of being a shepherd.

The Shepherd is to Lead

The shepherd gave individual names to his sheep, he knew each one by name. The sheep would respond to the shepherd, ". . . and the sheep hear his voice: and he calleth his own sheep by name, and leadeth them out" (John 10:3). The sheep will follow their pastor, "And a stranger will they not follow, but will flee from him: for they know not the voice of strangers" (John 10:5) This is the success of any pastor, to lead his sheep. Trying to drive them will bring about rebellion. But if he leads in love the sheep will follow.

The Shepherd is to Feed

Feeding the flock of God will mean that the pastor is to obey the injunction to, "Study to shew thyself approved unto God, a workman that needeth not to be ashamed, rightly dividing the word of truth" (2 Timothy 2:15).

The Shepherd is to Correct and Comfort

Turnbull states: "The pastor must rebuke and console". And both must be done with compassion. He must 'lift up the hands which hang down, and the feeble knees; and make straight paths' for the feet of the flock (Hebrews 12:12-13). He must reclaim the wandering sheep. He must rejoice with those who rejoice, and weep with those who weep. He must become all things to all men as he seeks to lead them to the Saviour, and to enable them to walk in his will and way. Like the great Shepherd of the sheep he should become one with his people, apart from their sins, that under his leadership they all may 'come in the unity of the faith, and of the knowledge of the Son of God, unto a perfect man, unto the measure of the stature of the fulness of Christ' (Ephesians 4:13)" (p. 295).

The Shepherd is to Protect

In this day of many false doctrines and cults, as never before, the pastor must ever be on the alert. Every minister of Christ should be aware of the gravity of our time, and give heed to the Scripture's teaching. "Also of your own selves shall men arise, speaking perverse things, to draw away disciples after them" (Acts 20:30).

The Minister is to be Faithful

The minister's first responsibility is to God. He has been placed in this position by God and must answer to him for his faithfulness.

In these times of compromise of the Bible, it is a "must" that God-called men be faithful to the Bible — faithful to proclaim its teaching. Paul the apostle felt the need to be faithful when he said, "But I keep under my body, and bring it into subjection: lest that by any means, when I have preached to others, I myself should be a castaway" (1 Corinthians 9:27).

Jesus loved the Church and gave Himself for it. As ministers we should give ourselves in faithful service to the Church. Serving as "... an example of the believers, in word, in conversation, in charity, in spirit, in faith, in purity" (1 Timothy 4:12).

In the twenty-third Psalm, David speaks about what the Good Shepherd meant to him. This would be a good example for ministers to take, in looking over God's flock as under shepherds. In this chapter we see concern for each individual sheep. He gives rest to the sheep. He provides green pastures and still waters — gives refreshment and encouragement to the sheep — provides leadership and guidance for them. He gives instruction, training and discipline; he provides for goals and motivation. There is provided fellowship and friendship.

The minister is to shepherd God's flock so that they do not lack anything — a tremendous responsibility! This is why we feel men must be called before being ordained to the ministry. "Therefore, brethren, stand fast, and hold the traditions which ye have been taught, whether by word, or our epistle" (2 Thessalonians 2:15).

WORK OF THE MINISTRY

The work of the ministry is to be an involvement of the body of Christ. God gives gifts, "for the perfecting of the saints, for the work of the ministry, for the edifying of the body of Christ" (Ephesians 4:12). God gives gifts, "ministries" to all. Believers not only receive the Spirit from God, but likewise a gift from the Spirit to use in the service of Christ. No member is without a gift of some sort. Some have more than one gift. The question is: Have you discovered your particular gift and are you using it to the full potential? "For the gifts and callings of God are without repentance" (Romans 11:29). There does not appear to be any question that everyone will have to give an account to God for his gift. The Scripture says, "Neglect not the gift that is in thee.. ."(1 Timothy 4:14). "In more recent times there has arisen a renewed vision for the recognition and mobilization of every member of the Body of Christ in some form of ministry."

"Gradually the Church is beginning to appreciate the value of every member actively participating in the work of the Church. It is here that an understanding of the variety of ministries which exist in the Word of God provides the incentive to discover what ministry God has for the individual believer. Ministry in every sense is, and must be, the ministry of the whole Church, and of each of its members in particular. The New Testament presents the doctrine of the priesthood of all believers and with it the necessary equipment to fulfill the Church's God-given function" (Brewster, p. 95).

Something to Think About

What I Owe My Minister:

I owe him respect as the ambassador of God, sent to teach me a better way of living than the selfish, sordid existence I might be guilty of but for his guidance.

I owe him trust, that he may be free to serve the church unhampered by fault-finding and criticism. I owe my minister prayer, that God may make his services a blessing to every one with whom he comes in contact.

I owe my minister the protection of a kindly silence by refraining from repeating in his presence the slander of unkind gossip that would worry him and prevent him from doing his best.

I owe him enough of my time to help him in his work whenever he may need me.

I owe my minister consideration not to interrupt and hinder his work by financial worry.

I owe my minister my attention when I go to church, that he may not be annoyed by seeing by my careless, inattentive actions that I am not interested in what he is saying.

L. O. Dawson, in his autobiography, tells of an interesting service in a church that had just buried its pastor. On the following Sunday a memorial was held in his honor. A large congregation overflowed the house. One speaker told of his worth as a preacher, another told of his tender ministrations as a pastor, others spoke of him as a citizen, some thought of him as a neighbor, or father, and so on to the end. When it came his turn to speak, Brother Dawson spoke as follows: "All you have said of my dead brother is true. He was a man out of the ordinary and gave of his remarkable powers to your service without stint or reserve. But if you had, while he was yet alive, filled these pews as you have today, he would not now be dead. Empty pews broke his heart, and he did not know of the love of which you have been speaking. He died for the lack of the things you have today so beautifully said and done." More preachers die from broken hearts than from swelled heads.

SUMMARY

The ministry is not a vocation one selects for himself, but rather one for which he has received a Divine call. The minister is to study to show himself approved. He is to be an example of the believer. His life is to be above reproach, in living up to the qualifications given in 1 Timothy 3:1-7 and Titus 1:5-10.

The minister is to be completely dedicated to God and His service, faithful in all aspects of his ministry. He must lose his life in complete dedication to his calling. He is not to be lord over God's flock, but rather lead them in love. He is to shepherd the flock of God, that the Holy Spirit has made him an overseer. His motive in service is not to be out of compulsion but willingly. Neither should he court the temporary glory of men. For "when the chief Shepherd shall appear, ye shall receive a crown of glory that fadeth not away" (1 Peter 5:4). The minister should be considered in a broader sense than the ordained minister. If the Great Commission is to be carried out as our Lord would have it be, then everyone in the body must find his place and be faithful in his ministry to the Lord.

DISCUSSION QUESTIONS

1. Does God call men to special work?
2. Could a person have more than one gift of ministry?
3. What do you think of the qualifications for the ministry?
4. What should the relationship be between ministers?
5. Is one gift greater than the other?
6. Should the minister be concerned about methods and goals?
7. Is study important for a minister?
8. Why do you feel there is emphasis placed on all the ministries?
9. What is your feeling toward your minister?
10. Would you like to be a minister?

BOOKS RECOMMENDED FOR STUDY

Brewster, P. S. *Pentecostal Doctrine.* Gloucestershire, England: P. S. Brewster, 1976.

Fitzwater, P. B. *Christian Theology.* Grand Rapids: William B. Eerdmans, 1948.

Nelson, P. C. *Bible Doctrines.* Springfield: Gospel Publishing House, 1971.

Turnbull, Ralph G. *Baker's Dictionary of Practical Theology.* Grand Rapids: Baker Book House, 1967.

CHAPTER 6

WATER BAPTISM

Baptism in water is by immersion, and is a direct commandment of our Lord (Matthew 28:19), and is for believers only. The ordinance is a symbol of the Christian's identification with Christ in His death, burial and resurrection (Romans 6:4; Colossians 2:12; Acts 8:36-39).

The following recommendation regarding the water Baptismal formula is adopted, to wit:

"On the confession of your faith in the Lord Jesus Christ the Son of God, and by his authority, I baptize you in the name of the Father, and of the Son, and of the Holy Ghost. Amen."

The doctrine of water baptism is of great importance to all Christians in the Christian community. Views and interpretations of this ordinance vary. The meaning of baptism, the modes of baptism, and subjects of baptism must be considered. The view and doctrines of those in the Pentecostal movement are almost the same, except those who differ in formula, such as those who baptize in Jesus' name.

THE MEANING OF BAPTISM

Church Ordinance

Water baptism is an ordinance of the Church which is "ordained" by the Lord Himself. "Go ye therefore, and teach all nations, baptizing them in the name of the Father, and of the Son, and of the Holy Ghost" (Matthew 28:19). We also refer to this ordinance of the church as one of the sacraments (sacred acts) of the church. This sacrament is "an outward and visible sign of an inward and spiritual experience." Water baptism is an outward sign of what has already taken place in the heart of the believer. Having accepted Christ and His shed blood for one's salvation, the believer then becomes a candidate for water baptism.

The Significance of Baptism

As stated before, baptism is an outward act showing an inner experience. This act signifies the inner experience of the believer in relationship to Christ the Redeemer. Water baptism portrays the fundamentals of the gospel. Salvation comes through Christ's death, burial and resurrection. We are "Buried with him in baptism, wherein also ye are risen with him through the faith of the operation of God, who hath raised him from the dead" (Colossians 2:12).

The act of baptism shows that the believer is identified with Christ. By immersion we are saying "Christ died for our sins in order that this man might die to sin." When the believer rises from the water it says: "Christ rose from the dead in order that this man might live a new life in righteousness." Water baptism signifies that the believer has by faith put on Christ. He has the character of Christ, so that men may see Christ in him. By the rite of baptism, the convert is saying; I'm a new creature in Christ; I have taken on His nature. I intend by His grace to walk in His likeness.

The symbolism of the death, burial and resurrection of Christ, and the believer's new life in Him, is further given by Paul, "Know ye not, that so many of us as were baptized into Jesus Christ were baptized into his death? Therefore we are buried with him by baptism into death: that like as Christ was raised up from the dead by the glory of the Father, even so we also should walk in newness of life. For if we have been planted together in the likeness of his death, we shall be also in the likeness of his resurrection" (Romans 6:3-5).

Baptism, then, means the enthronement of Christ as Lord of the believer's life. The disciples of Christ were to be brought under the authority of the Triune God. "Go ye therefore, and teach all nations, baptizing them in the name of the Father, and of the Son, and of the Holy Ghost" (Matthew 28:19). Those who were brought under the authority of Christ were taught the things He commanded. This teaching is an ever-pressing need.

We do not believe that baptism constitutes conversion or conveys regeneration, but it would be wrong to say it is not important as an act required by God. First it was commanded of Jesus (Matthew 28:19). Second, it was required by the early church of those responding to the gospel (Acts 2:38).

While baptism is not essential to salvation, it is essential to full Christian obedience. In the waters of baptism, the believer ratifies His commitment to Christ and God confirms through the inner witness of the Spirit His acceptance and approval of that faith. In this it becomes a means of grace and a source of great joy to those who meet its demands sincerely.

We may further state, if any should question the importance of water baptism, that our Lord himself submitted to water baptism, though He had no need of repentance, declaring that ". . . thus it becometh us to fulfill all righteousness" (Matthew 3:15).

THE MODES OF BAPTISM

Baptism is by Immersion

The Greek word *baptizo* means to dip, to immerse, or submerge. Baptism means immersion or submersion. Therefore we do not accept pouring or sprinkling as a Scripturally valid mode of baptism.

The study of the New Testament shows that believers were to be baptized, and gives the way in which it is to be done. The reader should consider the following closely, as it established the mode of baptism.

Water is required for baptism. "And as they went on their way, they came unto a certain water: and the eunuch said, See, here is water; what doth hinder me to be baptized?" (Acts 8:36).

Much water was required. "And John also was baptizing in Aenon near to Salim, because there was much water there: and they came, and were baptized" (John 3:23).

Both the administrator and the candidate went down into the water. "And he commanded the chariot to stand still: and they went down both into the water, both Philip and the eunuch; and he baptized him" (Acts 8:38).

The candidate was to be buried in water. "Buried with him in baptism, wherein also ye are risen with him through the faith of the operation of God, who hath raised him from the dead" (Colossians 2:12).

There was also a coming up out of the water. "And Jesus, when he was baptized, went up straightway out of the water: and, lo, the heavens were opened unto him, and he saw the Spirit of God descending like a dove, and lighting upon him" (Matthew 3:16).

"And when they were come up out of the water, the Spirit of the Lord caught away Philip, that the eunuch saw him no more: and he went on his way rejoicing" (Acts 8:39). Nelson says in *Bible Doctrines:* "As most great scholars of all branches of Christendom, even those who practice infant baptism and sprinkling and pouring, specifically declare, the original mode was immersion, as the Greek words translated "baptism" and "baptize" clearly signify. Moreover, nearly all the translations into modern languages convey the same meaning. It is no more difficult for a Greek scholar to tell you the meaning of the words used in the Greek New Testament for this ordinance than it is for an Englishman to tell the meaning of the words 'dip' or 'immerse' " (pp 60, 61).

THE SUBJECTS OF BAPTISM

Believers, Born Again

The subjects or candidates for water baptism are those who have believed on the Lord Jesus Christ as Savior. The Scripture teaches that the sinner must repent and believe. "... The time is fulfilled, and the kingdom of God is at hand: Repent ye, and believe the gospel" (Mark 1:15). "Then Peter said unto them, Repent, and be baptized every one of you ..." (Acts 2:38). When Philip was preaching in Samaria they believed and "... they were baptized, both men and women" (Acts 8:12). Saul was converted on the road to Damascus. At Damascus he was prayed for "... and he received sight forthwith, and arose, and was baptized" (Acts 9:18). As Peter spoke to a group of Gentiles they received the Holy Ghost. Peter asks, "Can any man forbid water, that these should not be baptized, which have received the Holy Ghost as well as we?" (Acts 10:47). Does anyone question the salvation of this group? I would think not. Other examples are found in Acts 10:47, 48; 16:30-34.

Infant Baptism

Infants are not to be baptized, because the Scripture requires that repentance and faith are essential to baptism. Since infants do not have sins to repent of and cannot exercise faith, they are logically excluded from water baptism. Says Brewster: "Baptism outwardly expresses the inward cleansing effected by the Word and the Spirit (Ephesians 5:26; Titus 3:5) and the believer's identification with Christ in His death, burial and resurrection. It is a "sign and seal" of a transaction that has taken place in which God's grace and man's faith have committed themselves to each other. For this reason, Pentecostals cannot accept the implications of infant baptism. In the New Testament records, baptism is invariably associated with receiving the Word (Acts 2:41), believing on Christ (Acts 8:12, 37) and repentance (Acts 2:38), responses which an uncomprehending infant cannot make" (p. 84).

The practice most common among the Pentecostals is the dedication of infants to Christ. A brief ceremony with a dedication prayer, a prayer for the guidance of the parents to raise the infant to accept the Lord. Since the infants have no sins to repent of and cannot exercise faith, we feel that dedication is the acceptable thing to do.

THE IMPORTANCE OF WATER BAPTISM

Baptism is an external and visible rite, symbolizing an inner and invisible experience. This inner experience is union with Christ. "For ye are all the children of God by faith in Christ Jesus. For as many of you as have been baptized into Christ have put on Christ" (Galatians 3:26, 27). By observing this ordinance, as instituted by Christ, we honor His name and show our love for Him.

Baptism Identifies

Baptism identifies the believer with Christ. "Therefore we are buried with him in baptism into death: that like as Christ was raised up from the dead by the glory of the Father, even so we also should walk in newness of life. For if we have been planted together in the likeness of his death, we shall be also in the likeness of his resurrection" (Romans 6:4, 5).

Baptism Shows Obedience

When the believer follows the Lord in water baptism he is obeying Christ's command (Matthew 28:19). Then it can be said, the convert who refuses to be baptized following his conversion is in disobedience to our Lord's command. The convert should feel as our Lord Himself when He was baptized. "And Jesus answering said unto him, Suffer it to be so now for thus it becometh us to fulfill all righteousness. . ." (Matthew 3:15). Jesus set an example for us in that He was baptized. You must be baptized if you are to walk in complete obedience to Him.

The Formula

Our Lord gave His apostles the formula when He said, "Go ye therefore, and teach all nations, baptizing them in the name of the Father, and of the Son, and of the Holy Ghost" (Matthew 28:19).

This we Pentecostals feel as the most acceptable term when baptizing: "On the confession of your faith in the Lord Jesus Christ the Son of God, and by His authority, I baptize you in the name of the Father, and of the Son, and of the Holy Ghost. Amen."

SUMMARY

The doctrine of water baptism is one of great importance. Though we Pentecostals do not believe in baptism of regeneration, we do feel that it is not to be taken lightly. And the new convert should be baptized as soon as possible, for putting off following the Lord in baptism will bring one to a place of disobedience to Christ's command.

We believe that baptism by immersion is clearly taught in Scripture and that no other mode is acceptable.

The teaching of Scripture on this doctrine is that "believers, born again" are the subjects who are to be baptized — that repentance is necessary before baptism. Therefore, infants are not to be baptized, as they do not know what is meant by repentance or how to have faith.

The formula the Lord gave in Matthew 28:19 is the formula that should always be followed.

DISCUSSION QUESTIONS

1. What is water baptism?
2. Is water baptism a sacrament?
3. Is immersion important as a mode of baptism?
4. What do we mean when we say to be buried with Him in baptism?
5. Who is to be baptized?
6. Is it important to be baptized?
7. Can you give some Bible examples of water baptism?
8. Give some different views of water baptism.
9. Can you give Biblical support for immersion?
10. Should we baptize infants?

BOOKS RECOMMENDED FOR STUDY

Brewster, P. S. *Pentecostal Doctrine.* Gloucestershire, England: P. S. Brewster, 1976.

Fitzwater, P. B. *Christian Theology.* Grand Rapids: William B. Eerdmans, 1948.

Nelson, P. C., *Bible Doctrines.* Springfield: Gospel Publishing House, 1971.

Pearlman, Myer. *Knowing The Doctrines Of The Bible.* Springfield: Gospel Publishing House, 1937.

CHAPTER 7
HOLY SPIRIT BAPTISM

The Baptism of the Holy Ghost and fire (Matthew 3:11), is a gift from God, as promised by the Lord Jesus Christ to all believers in this dispensation, and is received subsequent to the new birth (John 14:16, 17; Acts 1:8; 2:4, 38, 39; 10:44-48). The Baptism of the Holy Ghost is accompanied with the speaking in other tongues as the Holy Spirit Himself gives utterance as the initial physical sign and evidence. (Acts 2:4).

The Holy Spirit and His work is a vast study. There are many aspects of the Holy Spirit's work in the life of the believer as well as in the Church. His work in creation, His work as Sanctifier, and His work as He administers the gifts of the Spirit are important study areas. This is to mention only a few, but our purpose in this study is to get a good look at the doctrine of "Holy Spirit Baptism." We Pentecostals use the King James Version "Holy Ghost" most frequently; however, there is no difference in the two terms "Holy Ghost" or "Holy Spirit" in the original text.

THE PROMISE OF THE HOLY GHOST

Promised by the Prophets

"And it shall come to pass afterward, that I will pour out my spirit upon all flesh; and your sons and your daughters shall prophesy, your old men shall dream dreams, your young men shall see visions: And also upon the servants and upon the handmaids in those days will I pour out my spirit" (Joel 2:28,29). Isaiah the prophet also says, "For I will pour water upon him that is thirsty, and floods upon the dry ground: I will pour my spirit upon thy seed, and my blessing upon thine offspring" (Isaiah 44:3).

Promised to Believers

The Scriptural promises that follow are definitely pointing to Pentecost. "In the last day, that great day of the feast, Jesus stood and cried, saying, If any man thirst, let him come unto me, and drink. He that believeth on me, as the scripture hath said, out of his belly shall flow rivers of living water" (John 7:37, 38).

Jesus speaking to His disciples gave promise of the Holy Spirit: "And I will pray the Father, and he shall give you another Comforter, that he may abide with you for ever; Even the Spirit of truth; whom the world cannot receive, because it seeth him not, neither knoweth him: but ye know him; for he dwelleth with you, and shall be in you" (John 14:16, 17).

Jesus speaks of His leaving and gives a promise to send another Comforter: "Nevertheless I tell you the truth; It is expedient for you that I go away: for if I go not away, the Comforter will not come unto you; but if I depart, I will send him unto you" (John 16:7).

Just before the ascension of our Lord, He leaves this promise: "And, behold, I send the promise of my Father upon you: but tarry ye in the city of Jerusalem, until ye be endued with power from on high" (Luke 24:49). "And, being assembled together with them, commanded them that they should not depart from Jerusalem, but wait for the promise of the Father, which, saith he, ye have heard of me" (Acts 1:4).

In his sermon on the day of Pentecost, Peter gave explanation as to the coming of the Holy Ghost, that it was in fulfillment to God's promise. "Therefore being by the right hand of God exalted, and having received of the Father the promise of the Holy Ghost, he hath shed forth this, which ye now see and hear" (Acts 2:33). As Peter continues his sermon, he states that the promise is for all believers, and not for the apostles or for the hundred and twenty only. It was to those present, "to you," to those absent and those yet to be born, "to your children," and "to all that are afar off," which surely includes you and me! "For the promise is unto you, and to your children, and to all that are afar off, even as many as the Lord our God shall call" (Acts 2:39).

The Promised Holy Ghost is a Gift

The Baptism of the Holy Ghost is not something you earn or that can be bought with a price. It is a gift of God. There was no question in Peter's mind when he said, ". . . ye shall receive the gift of the Holy Ghost" (Acts 2:38).

"The promise of the Father," is used different times, which indicates that it is God's gift. The Holy Ghost is a gift God wants all believers to have. "For John truly baptized with water; but ye shall be baptized with the Holy Ghost not many days hence" (Acts 1:5). This places great emphasis upon the necessity of the Spirit Baptism.

HOLY GHOST EXPERIENCE

The Baptism of the "Holy Ghost and fire" is a gift from God as promised by the Lord Jesus Christ to all believers in this dispensation. We have examined many Scriptures as proof of God's promise. Now let us consider this experience being received subsequent to the new birth.

The First Record

The first record of those having received the experience of the "Baptism of the Holy Ghost" is given in Acts, chapter two. We sometimes refer to this experience as "being filled with the Holy Spirit." "And they were filled with the Holy Ghost, and began to speak with other tongues, as the Spirit gave them utterance" (Acts 2:4). There is no question about this group having experienced the new birth before receiving this experience at Pentecost. This we Pentecostals believe to be the Scriptural pattern for the whole Church age. The Bible is our source in establishing the doctrine of the "Baptism in the Holy Ghost."

"The Bible is the most definite book that was ever written. That is one of the reasons why I love it. The Bible is definite about salvation; so definite that if a man is saved, and knows his Bible, and you put to him the question, 'Are you saved,' he will reply, in all humility and yet with equal confidence, 'Yes, God in His infinite mercy has saved even me.' The Bible is just as definite about the Baptism with the Holy Spirit; so definite that if a man has been 'baptized with the Holy Spirit,' and knows his Bible, and you put to him the question, 'Have you been baptized with the Holy Ghost?' he will reply, in all humility and yet with equal confidence and positiveness, 'Yes, God has seen fit to baptize even me with His Holy Ghost'" (Torrey, p. 111).

The Holy Spirit baptism is to be received after regeneration. So, it is as clear as language can possibly make it, that it is one thing to be born again and something further, something additional, to be baptized with the Holy Spirit.

The Samaritans

The next outpouring of the Holy Spirit is a result of the preaching of Philip the evangelist, to the city of Samaria. When word was received of the revival in Samaria, by the church at Jerusalem, they sent unto them Peter and John. When the apostles arrived, "Then laid they their hands on them, and they received the Holy Ghost" (Acts 8:17). This enduement of power was of the same charismatic character as that which appeared at Pentecost.

"And when Simon saw that through laying on of the apostles' hands the Holy Ghost was given, he offered them money, saying, Give me also this power, that on whomsoever I lay hands, he may receive the Holy Ghost" (Acts 8:18,19). No one can doubt from these words that there was an outward evidence of the reception of the Spirit. It does not seem plausible that a man of Simon's caliber would offer money for the ability to produce an invisible effect.

Paul's Experience

The conversion of Saul is recorded in Acts, chapter nine. When Ananias was sent by the Lord to pray for Saul, he did not question his conversion as he says, "... Brother Saul, the Lord, even Jesus, that appeared unto thee in the way as thou earnest, hath sent me, that thou mightest receive thy sight, and be filled with the Holy Ghost" (Acts 9:17).

Paul says of his speaking in tongues, "I thank my God, I speak with tongues more than ye all" (1 Corinthians 14:18). Ralph M. Riggs in

The Spirit Himself, comments on Paul's experience as well as the experience of the Gentiles at Ephesus and Corinth. "It cannot be said that this evidence of tongues was manifest only at the initial outpouring of the Spirit upon the Jews and the Gentiles. Paul was a Jew and was filled with the Holy Spirit and said, 'I thank my God I speak with tongues more than ye all' (1 Corinthians 14:18). The Gentiles at Ephesus likewise received the Holy Spirit and 'spake with tongues and prophesied' (Acts 19:6). The Gentiles at Corinth also received this same experience with the speaking in other tongues, for the 12th, 13th and 14th chapters of First Corinthians reveal this fact" (p. 88).

As seen in these Scriptures, the "Baptism of the Holy Ghost" is an experience received subsequent to the new birth.

The Initial Physical Evidence

In Acts, chapter two, the physical evidence that caused the fluster was that of speaking in tongues — "languages they had never learned" — a wonderful manifestation of God's power.

In the initial evidence of this charismatic impartation of the Holy Ghost, there is always an immediate, supernatural, outward expression, convincing not only the receiver but the people listening to him, that a divine power is controlling the person; and in every case there is an ecstatic speaking in a language that the person has never learned.

In the early Church, the receiving of the Baptism of the Holy Ghost was no formal ceremony or doctrinal theory, but a real experience — an experience that was definite and observable. The examination of Scripture on this great doctrinal subject we believe proves that all who receive the Baptism in the Spirit today also speak with tongues.

The Experience Changes One's Life

Once a person has received the initial infilling of the Holy Spirit, he does not stop with being filled, he lives a victorious life. Different phases of the experience are evident: There is the initial filling when a person is first baptized with the Holy Spirit. A habitual condition is referred to in the words, "full of the Holy Ghost" (Acts 6:3; 7:55; 11:24), which words describe the daily life of a spiritual person, or one whose character reveals "the fruit of the Spirit." The habitual condition is referred to in the exhortation, "Be filled with the Spirit" (Ephesians 5:18).

There are also times of special fillings and anointings. There appears to be a special enduement for Paul to resist the power of a sorcerer (Acts 13:9). The same is true with Peter before the Jewish council (Acts 4:8).

THE IMPORTANCE OF HOLY SPIRIT BAPTISM

The Holy Ghost Empowers

The Holy Ghost empowers the believer in his personal life for witnessing. "But ye shall receive power, after that the Holy Ghost is come upon you: and ye shall be witnesses unto me both in Jerusalem, and in all Judea, and in Samaria, and unto the uttermost part of the earth" (Acts 1:8).

The study of the outpouring of the Holy Spirit in this twentieth century is certainly proof of His effectiveness in producing revival. T. W. Walker says this experience "Set off the Pentecostal explosion at the beginning of this century. Though revivals throughout Church history and particularly since the Reformation had seen the renewal of the outpouring of the Holy Spirit, it is true to say that nothing has been parallel to the worldwide penetration of

Pentecost since the early 1900s. Figures like 30,000,000 Pentecostal believers are frequently mentioned and the demand and demonstration of the power of the Holy Spirit within and outside the Pentecostal churches must be reckoned with on a rapidly expanding and developing scale" (Brewster, p. 30).

A truly Pentecostal church will want to know in its members an ongoing experience of the Holy Spirit's fullness, but it will also desire and be unsatisfied until it has a vibrant, living, dynamic witness to and of the living Saviour.

Gives Life to Worship

Anyone who is acquainted with the lively worship of times of revival throughout church history knows this has resulted when men drew close to God. "The Pentecostal Revival is no exception. Many believe that the seventy years or so of Pentecostal history are but our probationary period. Greater expansion is coming. Deeper worship is here. There is increasing evidence that churches that have not been part of the Pentecostal Movement are being transformed as members are baptized in the Spirit and the rivers of living water begin to flow" (Brewster, p. 41).

Today we are seeing a renewed interest in the Baptism of the Holy Spirit. People of many faiths are seeking and receiving this infilling. Many want to know: What does the Bible teach about this experience? We Pentecostals must be ready to teach this doctrine, for Jesus would have all men to " . . . worship him in spirit and in truth" (John 4:24).

HOW TO RECEIVE THE BAPTISM OF THE HOLY GHOST

The question is asked many times, How can I receive the Holy Ghost? The following should help answer the question and bring the seeker to a place of receiving.

A right attitude is essential. "These all continued with one accord in prayer and supplication, with the women, and Mary the mother of Jesus, and with his brethren" (Acts 1:14).

United prayers of the church. "And when they had prayed, the place was shaken where they were assembled together; and they were all filled with the Holy Ghost, and they spake the word of God with boldness" (Acts 4:31). When hearts are prepared there may be a spontaneous outpouring as was in the case of those in the house of Cornelius.

When you ask in faith, "If ye then, being evil, know how to give good gifts unto your children: how much more shall your heavenly Father give the Holy Spirit to them that ask him?" (Luke 11:13).

The seeker must obey. "And we are his witnesses of these things; and so is also the Holy Ghost, whom God hath given to them that obey him" (Acts 5:32). You must believe "...he that cometh to God must believe that he is, and that he is a rewarder of them that diligently seek him" (Hebrews 11:6). Askers, seekers, knockers after the Baptism in the Spirit, should always remember that this experience is also called, "The Gift of the Holy Ghost." Gifts are not earned or won by price or merit. Gifts cannot be forced from the giver.

Baptism of the Holy Spirit comes when there is a perfect yielding of the entire being to Him and one's tongue is surrendered to the control of the Holy Spirit.

SUMMARY

The Holy Ghost Baptism is a gift from God; it was promised by our Lord. The prophets prophesied of His coming. This promise was made to all believers.

The experience of the Baptism of the Holy Ghost is an experience received subsequent to the new birth. The Baptism of the Holy Ghost is accompanied with the speaking in other tongues. Tongues are the initial physical evidence of having received the Baptism of the Holy Ghost. A man may be regenerated by the Holy Ghost and never be baptized in the Holy Ghost. In regeneration there is an importance of life, significant of salvation; in the baptism of the Holy Ghost there is an infilling of power, significant of service and witnessing.

The infilling of the Holy Ghost empowers the recipient to be a strong witness for Christ. It gives the believer Holy boldness. The one who hungers after righteousness is filled with a desire to worship his Saviour. When one is filled with the Holy Ghost, worship and praise come easily. The Baptism of the Holy Ghost can be received by every Christian who will ask Him in faith and follow Him in complete obedience.

DISCUSSION QUESTIONS

1. Is the Holy Ghost a person?
2. Has God promised the Holy Ghost to every one?
3. Who may receive the Baptism of the Holy Ghost?
4. Is the Holy Ghost something you work for?
5. What is the initial physical evidence of the Baptism of the Holy Ghost?
6. Does the Holy Ghost have an effect on one's life?
7. Can you give some symbols of the Holy Ghost?
8. Do all speak in tongues?
9. What does it mean to be filled with the Spirit?
10. Do you have the Baptism of the Holy Ghost?

BOOKS RECOMMENDED FOR STUDY

Brewster, P. S. *Pentecostal Doctrine.* Gloucestershire, England: P. S. Brewster, 1976.

Brumback, Carl. *What Meaneth This?* Springfield: Gospel Publishing House, 1947.

Pearlman, Myer. *Knowing The Doctrines Of The Bible.* Springfield: Gospel Publishing House, 1937.

Riggs, Ralph M. *The Spirit Himself.* Springfield: Gospel Publishing House, 1949.

CHAPTER 8
SANCTIFICATION

The Bible teaches that without holiness no man can see the Lord (Hebrews 12:14). We believe in the doctrine of sanctification as a definite, yet progressive, work of grace, commencing at the time of regeneration and continuing until the consummation of salvation (Hebrews 13:12; 2 Thessalonians 2:13; 1 Peter 1:2; Ephesians 5:26; 1 Corinthians 6:11; John 17:17; 1 Thessalonians 5:23).

MEANING OF SANCTIFICATION

The primary meaning of sanctification is to dedicate, or set apart for God's use. Sanctification, holiness, and consecration are synonymous terms — terms that signify setting apart for a sacred purpose.

In the Mosaic system there were: 1) Sacred persons, such as the high priest, 2) Sacred things, as the tabernacle, and 3) Sacred seasons, such as the Passover and the Day of Atonement (Jeremiah 1:5; Leviticus 8:10).

The Christian is to be Set Apart for Christ

Paul, writing to the Corinthians, says: "Wherefore come out from among them, and be ye separate, saith the Lord, and touch not the unclean thing; and I will receive you" (2 Corinthians 6:17). Instruction is given that the Christian is to "Follow peace with all men, and holiness, without which no man shall see the Lord" (Hebrews 12:14).

To be sanctified, one is to dedicate himself to God and separate his life from a sinful world. In sanctification we are to "... cleanse ourselves from all filthiness of the flesh and spirit, perfecting holiness in the fear of God" (2 Corinthians 7:1).

MEANS OF SANCTIFICATION

How are men sanctified? This doctrine is explained very clearly in Scripture. The following gives us the Bible teaching of the means of sanctification.

Sanctified by God

"Sanctify them through thy truth: thy word is truth" (John 17:17). "And the very God of peace sanctify you wholly; and I pray God your whole spirit and soul and body be preserved blameless unto the coming of our Lord Jesus Christ" (1 Thessalonians 5:23).

Sanctified by Jesus Christ

"Husbands, love your wives, even as Christ also loved the church, and gave himself for it; That he might sanctify and cleanse it with the washing of water by the word" (Ephesians 5:25, 26). "By the which will we are sanctified through the offering of the body of Jesus Christ once for all" (Hebrews 10:10). "Wherefore Jesus also, that he might sanctify the people with his own blood, suffered without the gate" (Hebrews 13:12).

Sanctified by the Holy Spirit

"But we are bound to give thanks always to God for you, brethren beloved of the Lord, because God hath from the beginning chosen you to salvation through sanctification of the Spirit and belief of the truth" (2 Thessalonians 2:13). "Elect according to the foreknowledge of God the Father, through sanctification of the Spirit, unto obedience and sprinkling of the blood of Jesus Christ: Grace unto you, and peace, be multiplied" (1 Peter 1:2).

Sanctified Through the Word of God

"Sanctify them through thy truth: thy word is truth" (John 17:17). The Word of God shows the right way of life for the believer and gives the personal impulse and the energy to conform to God's righteous standard.

WHEN SANCTIFICATION TAKES PLACE

Sanctification takes place at the time one believes in Jesus Christ. He is saved; born again and sanctified. This is a definite, instantaneous work of grace. Paul says, "But we are bound to give thanks always to God for you, brethren beloved of the Lord, because God hath from the beginning chosen you to salvation through sanctification of the Spirit and belief of the truth" (2 Thessalonians 2:13).

"When we believe on the Lord Jesus Christ and accept Him as our Savior, we are justified by faith in Him and stand before God without any condemnation on our souls; we are regenerated, that is, born again through the operation of the Holy Spirit and the Word of God, and have become new creatures. 'We are also separated from sin and cleansed and purged by the blood of Jesus' (1 John 1:7), and by our own will we set ourselves apart to the service of God, and Christ is now our 'wisdom, and righteousness, and sanctification, and redemption' (1 Corinthians 1:30). For this reason, all believers are designated 'saints' in the New Testament, and Paul addresses the Corinthian believers who were far from perfect as 'sanctified' (1 Corinthians 1:2)" (Nelson, p. 95).

Sanctification is a Progressive Work

In this secondary sense of sanctification there is a growth. "But we all, with open face beholding as in a glass the glory of the Lord, are changed into the same image from glory to glory, even as by the Spirit of the Lord" (2 Corinthians 3:18). "And he gave some, apostles; and some, prophets; and some, evangelists; and some, teachers; For the perfecting of the saints, for the work of the ministry, for the edifying of the body of Christ" (Ephesians 4:11-12). In the next verse Paul's emphasis is on growth. "Till we all come in the unity of the faith, and of the knowledge of the Son of God, unto a perfect man, unto the measure of the stature of the fulness of Christ" (Ephesians 4:13). Instructions from Peter are the same. "But grow in grace, and in the knowledge of our Lord and Savior Jesus Christ. To him be glory both now and for ever. Amen" (2 Peter 3:18). The believer set apart by God, advances in knowledge and grace. In the measure, therefore, that he acquires a fuller knowledge of the way of life and exercises in active service for God he advances in righteousness and true holiness. This progressive work is indicated by Paul when he says, "Being confident of this very thing, that he which hath begun a good work in you will perform it until the day of Jesus Christ" (Philippians 1:6).

In progressive sanctification there is an increasing hatred of sin. In progressive sanctification there is a growing interest in the things of God. The Psalmist says, "... his delight is in the law of the Lord; and in his law doth he meditate day and night" (Psalm 1:2). "The statutes of the Lord are right, enlightening the eyes" (Psalm 19:8). He further says of God's statutes, "More to be desired are they than gold, yea, than much fine gold: sweeter also than honey and the honeycomb" (Psalm 19:10).

In progressive sanctification there will be a desire for His word. "As newborn babes, desire the sincere milk of the word, that ye may grow thereby" (1 Peter 2:2). In progressive sanctification there will be a greater love for heavenly things. Paul in his letter to the Colossians writes, "If ye then be risen with Christ, seek those things which are above, where Christ sitteth on the right hand of God. Set your affection on things above, not on things on the earth. For ye are dead, and your life is hid with Christ in God. When Christ, who is our life, shall appear, then shall ye also appear with him in glory" (Colossians 3:1-4).

Having once been cleansed (sanctified) through regeneration, the Christian has the responsibility of progressing, as we see from the following Scriptures. "Having therefore these promises, dearly beloved, let us cleanse ourselves from all filthiness of the flesh and spirit, perfecting holiness in the fear of God" (2 Corinthians 7:1). "I speak after the manner of men because of the infirmity of your flesh: for as ye have yielded your members servants to uncleanness and to iniquity unto iniquity; even so now yield your members servants to righteousness unto holiness" (Romans 6:19). "But now being made free from sin, and become servants to God, ye have your fruit unto holiness, and the end everlasting life" (Romans 6:22).

"Many other Scriptures portray this important aspect of holiness. These Scriptures prove conclusively that, though we are made holy, holiness has to be developed. Our whole personality needs cultivation and this cultivation produces progressive sanctification. This is why it is called 'fruit.' The fruit is produced by the root and, if this root is neglected, then the fruit will show it. 'I am the vine, ye are the branches . . . without me ye can do nothing ... If a man abide not in me... he is withered.' If we keep stating and acting as if the positional and innate nature is enough and that we need do no more, we deny the One who gave us the gift of holiness" (Brewster, p. 363).

WHAT ABOUT CHRISTIAN PERFECTION?

Perfection is a term we use often. A perfect line, a perfect tree, a perfect apple, or a perfect whatever. These references are used to make our meaning clear and definite. Christian perfection is not absolute perfection; this belongs to God only. In this sense, " ... there is none good but one, that is, God ..." (Matthew 19:17). Purity and maturity! These words are similar in sound, but they are very distinct in meaning. Purity is found when a soul finds pardon and peace with God, but maturity involves time, growth, trial and development.

Says Brewster, "We must give attention to the cultivation of the spiritual nature through instruction which will direct us in our service Godward and menward. The truth must first sanctify us and then it will sanctify others. 'For their sakes I sanctify myself.' If we neglect to develop the nature of holiness which is given to us at regeneration by failure to cultivate the life which we have from Christ, we will be totally unable to have the power to reproduce. This is one major reason why there is poverty in the lives of so many individuals in our congregations. They do not grow, simply because they do not develop, nourish and cultivate that holy nature" (p.363)

SUMMARY

Sanctification is both absolute and progressive. Sanctification as an instantaneous act cleanses us from all sin, and brings us to a place of obedience. Walking in the light of obedience, we are recipients of a progressive or continuous sanctification.

We believe that a person is sanctified when converted. That he has been washed clean by the blood of Christ. We also are to ". . . grow in grace, and in the knowledge of our Lord and Savior Jesus Christ" (2 Peter 3:18). The destruction of sin in the soul, and the growth of holiness are two distinct things. The one is instantaneous, the other is gradual. Though there is a difference of opinion among Pentecostals in regard to method of sanctification, all believe in a holy life.

DISCUSSION QUESTIONS

1. What is meant by sanctification?
2. How is a person sanctified?
3. When is one sanctified?
4. Is sanctification a work of grace?
5. What is meant by progressive sanctification?
6. What happens in progressive sanctification?
7. Can a Christian be perfect?
8. What does it mean to grow in grace?
9. Can a person sanctify himself?
10. Can things be sanctified?

BOOKS RECOMMENDED FOR STUDY

Brewster, P. S. *Pentecostal Doctrine.* Gloucestershire, England: P. S. Brewster, 1976.

Fitzwater, P. B. *Christian Theology.* Grand Rapids: Zondervan Publishing House, 1948.

Nelson, P. C. *Bible Doctrines.* Springfield: Gospel Publishing House, 1971.

Pearlman, Myer. *Knowing The Doctrines Of The Bible.* Springfield: Gospel Publishing House, 1937.

CHAPTER 9

THE LORD'S SUPPER

The ordinance of the Lord's Supper is a commandment of our Saviour; and, being a memorial to His death and resurrection, is strictly limited to Christian believers (1 Corinthians 11:27). Its time and frequency of observance is left to the discretion of each congregation. (1 Corinthians 11:26).

Only unfermented grape juice, the fruit of the vine, as recommended by our Lord (Matthew 26:29; Mark 14:25; Luke 22:18) shall be used in connection therewith.

The Lord's Supper is also referred to as the Holy Communion and a sacrament. When one is mentioned it is the same as the other. This holy ordinance symbolizes the broken body and the shed blood of our Lord Jesus Christ. This memorial of Christ's death looks forward to His coming again. This sacred rite was instituted by our Lord and is to be observed by Christians only.

ORDINANCE

The Lord's Supper is an ordinance of the Church, commanded by our Lord Jesus Christ. "And he took bread, and gave thanks, and brake it, and gave unto them saying, This is my body which is given for you: this do in remembrance of me" (Luke 22:19).

The importance of the observance of the Lord's Supper is given by the apostle Paul in 1 Corinthians 11:17-34. The ordinance is to be observed in remembrance of Christ's death and resurrection. "For as often as ye eat this bread, and drink this cup, ye do shew the Lord's death till he come" (1 Corinthians 11:26).

THE ELEMENTS

The elements used in the Lord's Supper by Pentecostals and most Evangelicals is unfermented grape juice and unleavened bread. Jesus said, "But I say unto you, I will not drink henceforth of this fruit of the vine..." (Matthew 26:29). Jesus also refers to the fruit of the vine in Mark's gospel. "Verily I say unto you, I will drink no more of the fruit of the vine, until that day that I drink it new in the kingdom of God" (Mark 14:25). Luke states, "For I say unto you, I will not drink of the fruit of the vine, until the kingdom of God shall come. And he took bread, and gave thanks, and brake it, and gave unto them saying, This is my body which is given for you: this do in remembrance of me. Likewise also the cup after supper, saying, This cup is the new testament in my blood, which is shed for you" (Luke 22:18-20). As we see from these Scriptures, certainly the most fitting would be unleavened bread and unfermented juice of the grape.

Erroneous Views

Transubstantiation. That the elements are changed into the actual body and blood of Christ. This could not be true as Christ was alive and with the disciples when he instituted the ordinance of the Lord's Supper. "And as they were eating, Jesus took bread, and blessed it, and brake it, and gave it to the disciples, and said, Take, eat; this is my body. And he took the cup, and gave thanks, and gave it to them, saying, Drink ye all of it; For this is my blood of the new testament, which is shed for many for the remission of sins" (Matthew 26:26-28).

"When Christ made this declaration, He was physically present with the disciples. He had not yet been crucified. It must, therefore, mean that the elements represent or symbolize Christ's body and His blood. Transubstantiation involves the denial of the completeness and fulness of Christ's atonement. It furthermore implies the blasphemous assumption that a sinful man can add anything to Christ's atoning work" (Fitzwater, p. 490).

Consubstantiation. This view declares Christ's bodily presence in the elements of the communion. This is also to be rejected as erroneous doctrine. As I understand the doctrine of consubstantiation, it makes the reception of Christ's saving grace dependent upon contact with that which is matter, whereas, the Scripture asserts that the righteousness of Christ is received by faith. "Whom God hath set forth to be a propitiation through faith in his blood, to declare his righteousness for the remission of sins that are past, through the forebearance of God" (Romans 3:25). "And they said, Believe on the Lord Jesus Christ, and thou shalt be saved, and thy house" (Acts 16:31).

The Elements are Symbols

The bread is a symbol of His broken body

"And as they were eating, Jesus took bread, and blessed it, and brake it, and gave it to the disciples, and said, Take, eat; this is my body" (Matthew 26:26). Bread "the staff of life" is the most appropriate symbol that could be used. Jesus said, "I am that bread of life. Your fathers did eat manna in the wilderness, and are dead. This is the bread which cometh down from heaven, that a man may eat thereof, and not die. I am the living bread which came down from heaven: if any man eat of this bread, he shall live for ever: and the bread that I will give is my flesh, which I will give for the life of the world" (John 6:48-51).

The fruit of the vine is the symbol of Christ's shed blood

"But I say unto you, I will not drink henceforth of this fruit of the vine. . ." (Matthew 26:29).

The elements symbolize union of the Christians with Christ. "The cup of blessing which we bless, is it not the communion cup of the blood of Christ? The bread which we break, is it not for communion of the body of Christ? For we being many are one bread, and one body: for we are all partakers of that one bread" (1 Corinthians 10:16, 17).

There also is the symbolizing of the coming joy of the kingdom of God. ".. .until that day when I drink it new with you in my Father's kingdom" (Matthew 26:29).

RECEIVING COMMUNION

Who is to Receive Communion?

Those who are regenerated — born again. "But the natural man receiveth not the things of the Spirit of God: for they are foolishness unto him: neither can he know them, because they are spiritually discerned" (1 Corinthians 2:14). "Jesus answered and said unto him, Verily, verily, I say unto thee, Except a man be born again, he cannot see the kingdom of God. Nicodemus saith unto him, How can a man be born when he is old? can he enter the second time into his mother's womb, and be born? Jesus answered, Verily, verily, I say unto thee, Except a man be born of water and of the Spirit, he cannot enter into the kingdom of God" (John 3:3-5).

An Orderly Walk

Those who partake of the Lord's table should be walking orderly. Holy living is an essential qualification entitling one to sit at the Lord's table. An orderly walk is the proof of a saved life. Those receiving should prepare their hearts. "But let a man examine himself, and so let him eat of that bread, and drink of that cup. For he that eateth and drinketh unworthily, eateth and drinketh damnation to himself, not discerning the Lord's body. For this cause many are weak and sickly among you, and many sleep" (1 Corinthians 11:28-30). The exhortation is not to examine one's self and then remain away from the Lord's table, but to examine one's self and prepare his heart and then eat.

Healing in Receiving Communion

"If you are sick or afflicted in your body and can discern the healing virtue in the body of our Lord, typified by the bread, you may receive healing and strength for your body as well as for your spiritual nature" (1 Corinthians 11:30-32). If the true significance of the sacrifice of the body of Christ was discerned, many would be healed. "But he was wounded for our transgressions, he was bruised for our iniquities: the chastisement of our peace was upon him; and with his stripes we are healed" (Isaiah 53:5). Our Lord suffered the stripes on His body that we might be healed.

Fellowship in Communion

The words of our Lord reveal the yearning of His heart toward His own. " . . . With desire I have desired to eat this passover with you before I suffer" (Luke 22:15). The atmosphere of the upper room was filled with Christ's love for His disciples (John 13:1). This was a love which not only desired to eat with them, but to minister to them in the washing of their feet. He also looked forward to the time He would feast again with them in His Father's kingdom. The Lord's table is a place of togetherness, a place of fellowship.

"Our common meal together with Him speaks of the fact that we are 'in this together.' His death is for us and by faith we are reckoned to be crucified with Him. We are participants in His body and blood because we are one with Him through grace on His part and faith on ours. The communion He offers us each time we come to the Table not only signifies an event in which we were once united, but also a continuing relationship" (Brewster, p. 88).

Paul speaks of fellowship of the Church as he says, "For we being many are one bread, and one body: for we are partakers of that one bread" (1 Corinthians 10:17). Here we have fellowship with Christ and also enjoy fellowship with fellow-believers.

"The Lord's Supper thus embraces every dimension. It looks backward to the cross, upward to the throne of God, outward to the fellowship of saints and forward to the coming of the King, and so it becomes the focal point where grace encounters faith and assures us that past, present and future are held in the mighty hand that . . . [served His disciples the first communion]" (Brewster, p. 89).

How Often Should We Receive Communion?

The Scriptures do not say how often. The instruction is, ". . . as oft as you drink it, in remembrance of me" (1 Corinthians 11:25). A common practice among Pentecostals is to set the first Sunday of the month aside for communion.

SUMMARY

"The Lord's Supper" is a solemn moment. A moment when we remember His death for our sins. His body broken, His blood shed, as He was nailed to the cross. Yes, "The Lord's Supper" reminds us of the greatest event that has ever taken place. In serving the elements of communion, only unfermented grape juice, the fruit of the vine, should be served. This important truth should echo and re-echo throughout the Christian church, that "The Lord's Supper" is a memorial service. The whole idea in its observance is the commemoration of Christ's death.

DISCUSSION QUESTIONS

1. What is the Lord's Supper?
2. Is the communion an ordinance of the Church?
3. What are the elements used in communion?
4. What is the doctrine of transubstantiation?
5. What does communion symbolize?
6. Who is to receive communion?
7. How often should communion be served?

8. What is the general practice of Pentecostals in how often they serve communion?

9. How often do you feel communion should be served?

10. What is meant by closed communion?

BOOKS RECOMMENDED FOR STUDY

Brewster, P. S. *Pentecostal Doctrine*. Gloucestershire, England: P. S. Brewster, 1976.

Nelson, P. C. *Bible Doctrine*. Springfield: Gospel Publishing House, 1971.

Pearlman, Myer. *Knowing The Doctrines Of The Bible*. Springfield: Gospel Publishing House, 1937.

Turnbull, Ralph G. *Baker's Dictionary Of Practical Theology*. Grand Rapids: Baker Book House, 1967.

CHAPTER 10
DIVINE HEALING

Healing is for the physical ills of the human body and is wrought by the power of God, through the prayer of faith, and by the laying on of hands (Mark 16:18; James 5:14-15); it is provided for in the atonement of Christ, and is available to all who truly believe.

The Scriptures dealing with the doctrine of divine healing are abundant. It would be impossible to cover all Scripture dealing with divine healing in one short study, so we will try to touch some highlights on this large subject. This doctrine has been one that the Pentecostal movement has emphasized. A sensible understanding of this particular doctrine will lead us to praise, to faith and to rejoicing in the goodness of God's provision.

PHYSICAL HEALING

The doctrine of healing is one that all Pentecostals believe. But, it certainly isn't limited to the Pentecostals. Many Christians believe in the healing of the sick through the prayer of faith. Anyone can find many Christians who have proof in their own bodies.

Healing in the Atonement

The Christian community, in the most part, accepts the shed blood of Christ as the atonement for their sins. For it is stated by the writer in Hebrews, ". . . without shedding of blood is no remission" (Hebrews 9:22). In John's epistle, he says, "But if we walk in the light, as he is in the light, we have fellowship one with another, and the blood of Jesus Christ his Son cleanseth us from all sin" (1 John 1:7).

We feel that the Scripture teaches that in the atonement there is provision made for physical healing, as well as for deliverance from sin and its penalty. The prophet Isaiah connects physical healing with Christ's suffering. He says, "Surely he hath borne our griefs, and carried our sorrows: yet we did esteem him stricken, smitten of God, and afflicted. But he was wounded for our transgressions, he was bruised for our iniquities: the chastisement of our peace was upon him; and with his stripes we are healed" (Isaiah 53:4, 5).

Jesus healed Peter's mother-in-law, and the same day He cast out devils, and healed all that were sick. "That it might be fulfilled which was spoken by Isaiah the prophet, saying, Himself took our infirmities, and bare our sicknesses" (Matthew 8:17). This was done in fulfillment to the prophecy that was dealing with Christ's suffering for the sin of the world. But, in His suffering, His stripes purchased our healing.

The apostle Peter, writing about this great promise of divine healing, makes the same connection between Christ's suffering for our sin and physical healing. "Who His own self bare our sins in his own body on the tree, that we, being dead to sins, should live unto righteousness: by whose stripes ye were healed" (1 Peter 2:24).

HEALING IN THE GOSPEL

The mission of the twelve whom Jesus sent forth to preach the kingdom of heaven was to include, "Heal the sick, cleanse the lepers, raise the dead, cast out devils: freely ye have received, freely give" (Matthew 10:8). The seventy that Jesus sent forth into the harvest field, He told, whatsoever city you enter into, ". . . heal the sick that are therein, and say unto them, the kingdom of God is come nigh unto you" (Luke 10:9).

Jesus Healed the Sick

The following are a few examples of Jesus' ministry of healing the sick: Jesus heals a leper: "And Jesus put forth his hand, and touched him, saying, I will; be thou clean. And immediately his leprosy was cleansed" (Matthew 8:3).

A centurion's servant healed: "And Jesus said unto the centurion, Go thy way; and as thou hast believed, so be it done unto thee. And his servant was healed in the selfsame hour" (Matthew 8:13). Peter's mother-in-law healed: "And when Jesus was come into Peter's house, he saw his wife's mother laid, and sick of a fever. And he touched her hand, and the fever left her: and she arose, and ministered unto them" (Matthew 8:14, 15).

Jesus heals a paralyzed man: "But that ye may know that the Son of man hath power on earth to forgive sins, (then saith he to the sick of the palsy,) Arise, take up thy bed, and go into thine house" (Matthew 9:6).

Woman with an issue of blood: "But Jesus turned him about, and when he saw her, he said, Daughter, be of good comfort; thy faith hath made thee whole. And the woman was made whole from that hour" (Matthew 9:22).

Two blind men received their sight: "Then touched he their eyes, saying, According to your faith be it unto you. And their eyes were opened; and Jesus straightly charged them saying, See that no man knows it" (Matthew 9:29, 30).

When John the Baptist was in prison, he sent two of his disciples to Jesus, to inquire of Jesus if he be the Christ or not. Jesus told them to tell John about the things they saw and heard: "The blind receive their sight, and the lame walk, the lepers are cleansed, and the deaf hear, the dead are raised up, and the poor have the gospel preached to them" (Matthew 11:5).

The Disciples' Mission

The mission of the twelve was to ". . . preach, saying, the kingdom of heaven is at hand. Heal the sick, cleanse the lepers, raise the dead, cast out devils: freely ye have received, freely give" (Matthew 10:7, 8).

The same is given to the seventy. "And into whatsoever city ye enter, and they receive you, eat such things as are set before you: And heal the sick that are therein, and say unto them, The Kingdom of God is come nigh unto you" (Luke 10:8, 9).

The believers are to have signs following them. The last words of Jesus before He ascended on high, according to Mark 16:18, are a perpetual promise of the healing power: "They (believers) shall lay hands on the sick, and they shall recover." The final instructions given believers through James 5:14 directs them when sick to "call for the elders of the church," who are to anoint them and pray over them, and to this the great promise is added: "The prayer of faith shall save the sick, and the Lord shall raise him up."(James 5:15).

After the ascension, the apostles were carrying out Christ's commission. "Insomuch that they brought forth the sick into the streets, and laid them on beds and couches, that at the least the shadow of Peter passing by might overshadow some of them" (Acts 5:15).

THE MINISTRY OF HEALING

The ministry of healing was given to the believers. ". . . they shall lay hands on the sick, and they shall recover" (Mark 16:18). This ministry of healing is for the church today. "Is any sick among you? let him call for the elders of the church; and let them pray over him, anointing him with oil in the name of the Lord" (James 5:14). This epistle of James is inspired, as "All scripture is given by inspiration of God, and is profitable for doctrine. . ." (2 Timothy 3:16).

"Some important teaching emerges from these scriptures. First, God can heal people without the aid of either man or medicine. Then, there is no sickness or disease which God cannot heal, irrespective of how long anyone has been afflicted. Thankfully, Jesus healed all manner of sickness. In one case a man had suffered for thirty-eight years before Christ instantly healed him (John 5:5). There is a sacred connection between the atoning work of Christ on the cross and divine healing. Christ's commission in all its fulness is for today. If it is right to go into all the world and preach the gospel today, it is right to go into all the world and lay hands on the sick for divine healing today. No mandate has ever been issued to tear out any section of the inspired command. Laying on of hands and anointing with oil are procedures ordained by God" (Brewster, pp. 201, 202).

Who May Be Healed?

Divine healing is for believers. "But Jesus said unto her, Let the children first be filled: for it is not meet to take the children's bread, and to cast it unto the dogs" (Mark 7:27).

Though Jesus states healing is for the children, He honors faith as we see in the following verses. "And she answered and said unto him, Yes, Lord: yet the dogs under the table eat of the children's crumbs. And he said unto her, For this saying go thy way; the devil is gone out of thy daughter. And when she was come to her house, she found the devil gone out, and her daughter laid upon the bed" (Mark 7:28-30).

Do All Receive Healing?

The answer to this question is evident, as there are many sick who have been prayed for and have not been healed. We do not always understand why some are healed and others are not.

"Many Christians have prayed for the Lord to spare their loved ones, but instead of their being healed, the Lord has taken them. Unfortunately, in some cases those left behind have become bitter. We must seek to comfort those who are bereaved and it is good for us to know that God knows exactly what He is doing and why He is doing it. Peter tried to stop the Master doing something, but Jesus insisted, saying: "What I do thou knowest not now, but thou shalt know hereafter" (John 13:7). What a comforting promise this is! Again, observe Isaiah 55:8, 9: "For my thoughts are not your thoughts, neither are your ways My ways, saith the Lord. For as the heavens are higher than the earth, so are My ways higher than your ways and My thoughts than your thoughts" (Brewster, pp. 207, 208).

When faith touches God, we can see miracles of healing today, as in the Bible days. But, genuine faith will cause us to trust God, regardless of how He answers our prayers. Peter, by a miracle from God, was delivered from prison, but James and Stephen were killed. Why? We do not know! This goes to prove that God's ways are so much higher than ours, that we should not ask, why? But rather have faith that says, "Though he slay me, yet will I trust in him . . ." (Job 13:15). True faith does not ignore God's sovereignty.

Even Christ was limited in His miracle working ability, by the unbelief of the people. "And he did not many mighty works there because of their unbelief " (Matthew 13:58). In his Journal, John Wesley records no less than two hundred forty cases of divine healing in connection with his ministry. If this divine gift was lost through unbelief, it is reasonable to expect it to be restored through faith.

Faith in God is not presumption or experiment. Faith that is based upon God's Word, believes that what He has said will come to pass. And like Abraham, "He staggered not at the promise of God through unbelief; but was strong in faith, giving glory to God; And being fully persuaded that, what he had promised, he was able also to perform" (Romans 4:20, 21). This quality of faith is unmovable, it keeps on believing God.

TESTIMONY

In 1970, I was admitted to the hospital for a herniated disc problem. After two weeks of intermittent traction, the decision was made that I would have surgery. I had all the prerequisites for surgery during the next six days. The morning before I was to have surgery, my doctor came to my room, his question, "All set to go for tomorrow?" My reply was, "I guess so." But as my doctor started to leave the room, he stopped at the foot of my bed. I said, "Doctor, if you were me, is this what you would do?" His reply was, "I wouldn't advise you to do anything that I wouldn't do myself." So I felt I was in good hands and said, "Doctor, I'm not trying to talk you out of surgery." He replied, "We can always do surgery. I'm going to the nurses' station and cancel your surgery." In a few days I was released to go home. Praise God, He heals today! To this day I haven't had surgery.

Many other times God has healed me as well as members of my family. During the years I've been in the ministry, I've seen many people healed by the divine power of God.

SUMMARY

We believe it is God's will to heal the sick. "When the even was come, they brought unto him many that were possessed with devils: and he cast out the spirits with his word, and healed all that were sick" (Matthew 8:16).

The apostles healed all who came to them. "There came also a multitude out of the cities round about unto Jerusalem, bringing sick folks, and them which were vexed with unclean spirits: and they were healed every one" (Acts 5:16).

All through the centuries, since the time of the apostles, there have been individuals who had faith in God for the healing of their bodies. And where New Testament faith is found, New Testament miracles will be wrought in the name of Jesus Christ.

We believe that, "Jesus Christ the same yesterday, and today, and forever" (Hebrews 13:8) applies to divine healing; that Jesus healed while here upon earth, and commissioned His disciples to heal the sick.

In this lesson we have dealt with divine healing; healing as a result of faith. We believe that God uses doctors and nurses to restore a person's health, and that there also is a natural process that is a result of divine healing.

DISCUSSION QUESTIONS

1. Is healing in the atonement?
2. What Scripture is used as proof of healing in the atonement?
3. Do all receive healing who are prayed for?
4. Give some reasons why some are not healed.
5. Is divine healing for Christians only?
6. Do you believe a sinner could be healed?
7. Should the church place more emphasis on healing?
8. How important is the laying on of hands in prayer for the sick?
9. Does God want His children to be healthy?
10. Give a personal testimony of healing.

BOOKS RECOMMENDED FOR STUDY

Brewster, P. S. *Pentecostal Doctrine.* Gloucestershire, England: P. S. Brewster, 1976.

Nelson, P. C. *Bible Doctrines.* Springfield: Gospel Publishing House, 1971.

Riggs, Ralph M. *The Spirit Himself.* Springfield: Gospel Publishing House, 1949.

CHAPTER 11

THE SECOND COMING OF CHRIST

The Bible promises, "This same Jesus shall so come in like manner." (Acts 1:11). His coming is imminent; when He comes, "The dead in Christ shall rise first: then we which are alive and remain shall be caught up together with them in the clouds to meet the Lord in the air." (1 Thessalonians 4:16-17). Following the tribulation, He shall return to earth, as King of kings, and Lord of lords, and together with His saints, who shall be kings and priests, He shall reign a thousand years (Revelation 20:6).

In this lesson we will deal with the two stages of "The Second Coming of Christ." First: the Rapture of the Church; Christ returning for His saints. Second: the revelation of Christ; when Christ returns with His saints to establish His kingdom on earth. The doctrine of "The Second Coming of Christ" is one of the most basic and emphasized doctrines in the Bible. Most Pentecostals believe in the pre-tribulation rapture of the Church. The majority of Pentecostal believers lay great stress on the coming of Christ *for* His saints then *with* His saints. We are to be as Paul says, "Looking for that blessed hope, and the glorious appearing of the great God and our Saviour Jesus Christ " (Titus 2:13).

THE RAPTURE

Rapture is a word that isn't used in the Bible. It is used to describe the catching away of the Church. Paul, referring to Christ descending from heaven, and the dead in Christ rising, first, says, "Then we which are alive and remain shall be caught up together with them in the clouds, to meet the Lord in the air: and so shall we ever be with the Lord" (1 Thessalonians 4:17). In verse sixteen of chapter four, Christ descends. In verse seventeen the Church is caught up. Here we see the bride meeting Christ in the air.

His Coming will be Sudden

"In a moment, in the twinkling of an eye, at the last trump: for the trumpet shall sound, and the dead shall be raised incorruptible, and we shall be changed" (1 Corinthians 15:52). We do not know when this will be, therefore we are to be ready. ". . . for in such an hour as ye think not the Son of man cometh" (Matthew 24:44).

His Coming will be Personal

When Christ was taken into heaven it was personal. "And when he had spoken these things, while they beheld, he was taken up; and a cloud received him out of their sight" (Acts 1:9). At this time the promise of Christ's personal return was given. . . this same Jesus, which is taken up from you into heaven, shall come in like manner as ye have seen him go into heaven" (Acts 1:11).

His Coming Literal and Visible

As we have seen from Acts, chapter 1 verses 10 and 11, Christ was literally and visibly caught up into heaven. Those who saw Him caught up were promised that He would return in like manner. Paul in referring to Christ's coming says, "For the Lord himself shall descend from heaven with a shout, with the voice of the archangel, and with the trump of God: and the dead in Christ shall rise first: Then we which are alive and remain shall be caught up together with them in the clouds, to meet the Lord in the air: and so shall we ever be with the Lord" (1 Thessalonians 4:16, 17).

WHEN WILL THE CHURCH BE RAPTURED?

We do not know the day or hour that Christ will come for His bride. We are told to "Watch therefore: for ye know not what hour our Lord doth come" (Matthew 24:42). Paul says, "For yourselves know perfectly that the day of the Lord so cometh as a thief in the night" (1 Thessalonians 5:2). In the gospel of Luke we are told to, "Be ye therefore ready also: for the Son of man cometh at an hour when ye think not" (Luke 12:40).

The clear teaching of Scripture is for all to be prepared for His return: "Teaching us that, denying ungodliness and worldly lusts, we should live soberly, righteously, and godly, in this present world; Looking for that blessed hope, and the glorious appearing of the great God and our Savior Jesus Christ" (Titus 2:12, 13).

His Coming Imminent

"But of that day and that hour knoweth no man, no not the angels which are in heaven, neither the Son, but the Father" (Mark 13:32). Since we know not what day or hour our Lord will return, this leads us to believe He could come any minute.

The writers of the New Testament as well as early Church fathers believed in the imminent return of Christ. "They held not only the premillennial view of Christ's coming, but also regarded that coming as imminent. The Lord had taught them to expect His return at any moment, and so they looked for Him to come in their day. Not only so, but they also taught His personal return as being immediate. The early Church lived in the constant expectation of their Lord's return, and hence was not interested in the possibility of a Tribulation period in the future" (Pentecost, p. 203).

The Rapture, being an event we believe to be imminent, is therefore pretribulational. Space does not permit us to deal in full with the Tribulation as the wrath of God and the seventieth week. Both of these events are important in relation to the end of this age; but primarily have to do with Israel instead of the Church. But attention should be considered to Paul's statement. "For God hath not appointed us to wrath, but to obtain salvation by our Lord Jesus Christ" (1 Thessalonians 5:9). "We are not looking for the Antichrist, or for the Tribulation. Our ears are attuned to hear the trumpet call of our Deliverer. Our eyes scan the skies, 'looking for that blessed hope, and the glorious appearing of the great God and our Savior Jesus Christ' (Titus 2:13). We are longing, looking and waiting for God's Son from Heaven (1 Thessalonians 1:10)" (Nelson, p. 30).

Setting a Time for the Lord's Return

We believe it is unwise to teach that the Lord will come at some specified time, thereby setting a date for His appearing and it is also unwise to teach, preach or publish visions of numbers and dates which would tend to fix the time of the second coming of the Lord.

Attempts have been made to set a time for Christ's return. As could be expected each time the attempts have been wrong. Yes! very wrong, for Christ has not yet come. Jesus says of His coming, "But of that day and hour knoweth no man, no, not the angels which are in heaven, neither the Son, but the Father" (Mark 13:32).

The blessed hope of the Church is the return of our Savior to gather us unto Himself, "And every man that hath this hope in him purifieth himself, even as he is pure" (1 John 3:3). Not knowing the time of Christ's coming to catch the Church away should cause His people to walk daily as though today may be the day. Praise God it may be!

THE RAPTURE CONTRASTED WITH CHRIST'S SECOND ADVENT

There is overwhelming Scriptural evidence in the difference in the Rapture and the Second Advent of Christ. When the Church is raptured, the dead are raised and we ". . . shall be caught up together with them in the clouds, to meet the Lord in the air . . ." (1 Thessalonians 4:17). Jude refers to Christ's coming with His saints in verse fourteen.

The contrast is between Christ coming *for* His saints and Christ coming *with* His saints. At the rapture, the saints go to heaven, while at the second coming saints remain in the earth without translation. At the rapture, the world is unchanged and unjudged and continues in sin, while at the second coming the world is judged and righteousness is established in the earth.

The rapture of the church is a deliverance from the day of wrath which follows, while the second coming is a deliverance of those who have believed in Christ during the time of trouble and have survived.

The rapture is always described as an event which is imminent, that is, could occur at any moment, while the second coming of Christ to the earth is preceded by many signs and events. The rapture of the saints is a truth revealed only in the New Testament while Christ's second coming to the earth with events preceding and following is a prominent doctrine of both testaments. The rapture relates only to those who are saved, while the second coming of Christ to the earth deals with both saved and unsaved. At the rapture Satan is not bound but is very active in the period which follows, while at the second coming Satan is bound and rendered inactive.

BETWEEN THE RAPTURE AND THE SECOND: ADVENT

The Judgment Seat of Christ

When the bridegroom comes and takes the bride away, He will take His bride to the marriage supper of the Lamb. Some time during this period ". . . we must all appear before the judgment seat of Christ; that every one may receive the things done in his body, according to that he hath done, whether it be good or bad" (2 Corinthians 5:10).

The Great Tribulation

Between the Rapture and the Second Advent of Christ will be the great tribulation here on the earth. As Pearlman states, "The Scriptures teach that the appearing of Christ ushering in the Millennial Age will be preceded by a troublous transition period characterized by physical disturbances, wars, economic difficulties, moral declension, religious apostasy, infidelity, and general panic and perplexity. The latter part of this transition period is known as the 'Great Tribulation,' a period during which the entire world shall be under the sway of an Anti-God and Anti- Christian government. Believers in God will be brutally persecuted, and the Jewish nation in particular will pass through the furnace of affliction" (p. 390).

The Scripture says, "For then shall be great tribulation, such as was not since the beginning of the world to this time, no, nor ever shall be" (Matthew 24:21).

THE SECOND ADVENT

The Second Advent is . . the coming of our Lord Jesus Christ with all his saints" (1 Thessalonians 3:13). This will be to set up His kingdom on the earth. John says, He "... hast made us unto our God kings and priests: and we shall reign on the earth" (Revelation 5:10). "... and shall reign with him a thousand years" (Revelation 20:6). "The Lord returns 'with' His Bride to execute judgment on the nations, to rule over the kingdoms of the world, to usher in God's reign on earth. The measure of the believer's share in executive rule will be commensurate with the degree of his faithfulness during his post-conversion period. It is then that 'he who has been faithful in little' will be rewarded with greater responsibilities. The Bride will share in the glories of her husband" (Brewster, p. 271).

Satan Bound

Satan is bound at the Second Advent of Christ. "And he laid hold on the dragon, that old serpent, which is the Devil, and Satan, and bound him a thousand years" (Revelation 20:2). Satan, the enemy of God and man who has been the agent in inducing man's rebellion against God, is now bound so that the human race may have a new opportunity to align itself with God and righteousness.

Christ's Reign for a Thousand Years

Many Old and New Testament passages combine their testimony that Christ will be the supreme ruler over the earth. Christ, as David's son, will sit upon the throne of David (2 Samuel 7:16; Psalm 89:20-37; Isaiah 11; Jeremiah 33:19-21). When Christ was born He came as a King, as announced by the Angel Gabriel to Mary (Luke 1:32, 33). As a King He was rejected (Mark 15:12, 13; Luke 23:20-24). When He was crucified He died as the King of the Jews (Matthew 27:37). In His second advent He is described as "KING

OF KINGS, AND LORD OF LORDS" (Revelation 19:16). Literally hundreds of verses in the Old Testament either state or imply that Christ will reign on earth. Some of the more important texts are especially clear (Isaiah 2:1-4; 9:6, 7; 11:1-10; 16:5; 24:23; 31:1; 40:1-11; 42:1-4; 52:7-15; 55:4; Daniel 2:44; 7:27; Micah 4:1-8; 5:2-5; Zechariah 9:9; 14:16,17).

SUMMARY

Christ's second coming is one of the most wonderful doctrines of the Bible. We are "looking for that blessed hope, and the glorious appearing of the great God and our Saviour Jesus Christ" (Titus 2:13).

He will first appear to catch His Bride away. This is what we call the "Rapture of the Church." The Rapture is imminent. We should be looking each day for His return. His return will be a literal, visible return. Jesus was taken into heaven in a cloud and He "... shall come in a like manner..." (Acts 1:11). We do not know the day or hour Christ will return. Therefore, it is wrong to set a time for His return.

When Christ returns for His Church, ". . . the dead in Christ shall rise first: Then we which are alive and remain shall be caught up together with them in the clouds, to meet the Lord in the air..." (1 Thessalonians 4:16,17). At this time He will take His Church to the marriage supper of the Lamb.

The Rapture of the Church is to take place before the Great Tribulation. "For God hath not appointed us to wrath, but to obtain salvation by our Lord Jesus Christ" (1 Thessalonians 5:9). We feel the wrath Paul refers to here is the Great Tribulation. This tribulation will last for seven years.

At the end of the tribulation, Christ returns with His saints, to set up His earthly kingdom. This reign will last for one thousand years. We shall rule and reign as kings and priests during this thousand years with Christ.

DISCUSSION QUESTIONS

1. Is the word Rapture found in the Bible?
2. What do we mean by Rapture?
3. When will the Rapture take place?
4. What is meant by Christ's return being pretribulational?
5. What is meant by the premillennial return of Christ?
6. Where will Christ return to earth?
7. Who will rule with Christ on the earth?
8. Who will appear at the Judgment Seat of Christ?
9. Can you give any signs of Christ's second coming?
10. Will Christ's second coming be bodily?

BOOKS RECOMMENDED FOR STUDY

Brewster, P. S. *Pentecostal Doctrine.* Gloucestershire, England: P, S. Brewster, 1976.

Nelson, P. C. *Bible Doctrines.* Springfield: Gospel Publishing House, 1971.

Pentecost, J. Dwight. *Things To Come.* Grand Rapids: Zondervan Publishing House, 1974.

Strombeck, J. F. *First the Rapture.* Moline, Illinois: Strombeck Agency, Inc., 1951.

CHAPTER 12

JUDGMENT

The one who physically dies in his sins without Christ is hopelessly and eternally lost in the lake of fire, and therefore has no further opportunity of hearing the Gospel or for repentance (Hebrews 9:27). The lake of fire is literal (Revelation 19:20). The terms "eternal" and "everlasting" used in describing the duration of the punishment of the damned (Matthew 25:41-46) in the lake of fire, carry the same thought and meaning of endless existence, as used in denoting the duration of joy and ecstasy of saints in the presence of God.

There are several Judgments mentioned in Scripture. There is Judgment of our sins, Judgment of Nations, the Judgment Seat of Christ, and the Final Judgment. There is not enough time to deal with all these judgments in one lesson. In this lesson we will deal with the unpleasant subject of the Final Judgment, which is the Judgment of the wicked. As the Christians are to be judged in a separate judgment, let us first consider briefly:

The Judgment Seat of Christ

This judgment is for the Christians. "For we must all appear before the judgment seat of Christ; that every one may receive the things done in his body, according to that he hath done, whether it be good or bad" (2 Corinthians 5:10). Brewster states: "The picture that he draws is taken from the Greek athletic festivals. After the races and the other competitions had finished, the judge or umpire sat upon his seat, from which he had watched all the events, and the winners of the various events appeared before him to receive their rewards" (Brewster, p 291).

This is not a question of the believers' final destiny, for this has already been settled. The purpose, we see, is to try each man's works. "For other foundation can no man lay than that is laid, which is Jesus Christ. Now if any man build upon this foundation gold, silver, precious stones, wood, hay, stubble; Every man's work shall be made manifest: for the day shall declare it, because it shall be revealed by fire; and the fire shall try every man's work of what sort it is. If any man's work abide which he hath built thereupon, he shall receive a reward. If any man's work shall be burned, he shall suffer loss: but he himself shall be saved; yet so as by fire" (1 Corinthians 3:11-15).

THE FINAL JUDGMENT

The Final Judgment or the Great White Throne Judgment is the place where the wicked are judged. It is here that the wicked are cast into hell. The doctrine of hell isn't a popular doctrine. It is one that we do not like to talk about. Though we may not like the thought of hell, we must face the fact that sin is to be punished. Unless there is repentance for sin, the sinner will be cast into hell.

Hell is a Real Place

Jesus talks about it as a place where . . the fire is not quenched" (Mark 9:44). A place where for those who are guilty of iniquity, He . . shall cast them into a furnace of fire; there shall be wailing and gnashing of teeth" (Matthew 13:42). Also, consider the "certain rich man" who cried to Abraham: "And he cried and said, Father Abraham, have mercy on me, and send Lazarus, that he may dip the tip of his finger in water, and cool my tongue; for I am tormented in this flame" (Luke 16:24).

This place is described as a lake of fire (Revelation 19:20). This is a place where John says: "And the smoke of their torment ascendeth up for ever and ever: and they have no rest day nor night" (Revelation 14:11). Hell is a place that is literal; a place of eternal suffering.

Hell is a place of separation from God. "Depart from me, ye cursed, into everlasting fire, prepared for the devil and his angels" (Matthew 25:41). If you have loved ones who are saved, they will be with Christ in heaven. So this means the lost also will be separated from loved ones. This separation is for eternity. The person who fails to accept Christ has damned himself to receive an eternity separated from God and those he has loved so dearly.

Hell is a place of memory. "But Abraham said, Son, remember . . (Luke 16:25). The rich man remembered the good things he had in this life. He remembered he had brothers. He did not want them to come to that place of torment. Since you have your memory in hell, you will remember mother's prayers. You will remember the encouragement that you have received from friends, and how they have encouraged you to serve Jesus. You will remember having attended church and the invitation given, and how you turned Christ down and did not come to Him. You will remember, but it will be too late. You will be in hell forever with your memory.

Hell is Eternal

Hell is referred to as "everlasting fire" (Matthew 25:41), "unquench-able fire" (Matthew 3:12; Luke 3:17), and the "fire that never shall be quenched" (Mark 9:43-45). Also, the description is used, "tormented day and night for ever and ever" (Revelation 20:10).

Satan may try to deceive men, and men may try to delude themselves into the belief that there is nothing alarming in the miseries of hell; but it is tremendously true that these miseries defy description and surpass adequate conception. It is particularly worthy of notice that the most awful things in the Bible concerning the punishment of the wicked are the words of Jesus. He was love incarnate, but he spoke of "outer darkness," "weeping, wailing, and gnashing of teeth," a "place of torment," "the worm that dieth not," "everlasting punishment," "eternal damnation" (Matthew 8:12; Luke 16:28; Matthew 25:46; Mark 3:29). All these are expressions of startling significance.

The place of punishment for the wicked is the unending burning in the lake of fire, which is the second death. "But the fearful, and unbelieving, and the abominable, and murderers, and whoremongers, and sorcerers, and idolators, and all liars, shall have their part in the lake which burneth with fire and brimstone: which is the second death" (Revelation 21:8).

Who Will go to Hell?

The sinners will go to hell. ". . . the soul that sinneth, it shall die" (Ezekiel 18:4). Paul, in writing to the Romans, says "For the wages of sin is death . . (Romans 6:23). When a person sins it is against God. God has said that sin is to be punished.

The unbelievers will go to hell. The Bible says that the unbelievers will have their part in the lake of fire (Revelation 21:8). Men may put Christ off, and not believe on Him, but some day they will believe in Him and then it will be too late.

Those who reject Christ will go to hell. Ford says, "To trample God's only begotten Son underfoot is the greatest sin that a man can commit. But you say, 'I do not drink — I do not curse — I have never committed adultery.' This is the sin that damns you: You have rejected Christ as your Saviour. If your name isn't written in the Lamb's book of life, you will be cast into the lake of fire. You may go through life saying, 'I am too busy with this world — I have no time for Christ.' At last you will have time to die, and you will wake up in hell because you have rejected the only way of salvation" (p. 121).

How One Can Escape Hell

The Scriptures teach that it takes repentance for sins in order for men to escape hell. "I tell you, Nay: but, except ye repent, ye shall all likewise perish" (Luke 13:3). "Repent ye therefore, and be converted, that your sins may be blotted out, when the times of refreshing shall come from the presence of the Lord" (Acts 3:19). "If we confess our sins, he is faithful and just to forgive us our sins, and to cleanse us from all unrighteousness" (1 John 1:9).

The Scriptures teach that men are to accept Christ as Savior. "For God so loved the world, that he gave his only begotten Son, that whosoever believeth in him should not perish, but have everlasting life" (John 3:16). And having accepted Him as Saviour, we are to confess Him before men. "Whosoever therefore shall confess me before men, him will I confess also before my Father which is in heaven" (Matthew 10:32).

After we have accepted Christ as our Saviour, we are to follow Him. "Be ye therefore followers of God, as dear children; And walk in love, as Christ also hath loved us, and hath given himself for us an offering and a sacrifice to God for a sweet smelling savor" (Ephesians 5:1, 2).

The one who will repent of his sins and accept Christ as Savior, then confess Him before men and follow Him as He leads, will escape the awful punishment of hell. "For the wages of sin is death; but the gift of God is eternal life through Jesus Christ our Lord" (Romans 6:23).

It is not God's will for you to go to hell. The Lord is "... not willing that any should perish, but that all should come to repentance" (2 Peter 3:9). The decision is yours. No one can make it for us. Hell was not prepared for men. It was .. prepared for the devil and his angels" (Matthew 25:41). No wonder the word of God states, "Behold, now is the accepted time; behold, now is the day of salvation" (2 Corinthians 6:2).

SUMMARY

The subject that involves teaching about the doctrine of hell is not easy; but one that must be taught, because lost men are going to be punished in hell.

The one who dies without having repented of his sins will be hopelessly lost in the lake of fire. This place, the Scriptures teach, is a literal lake of fire (Revelation 19:20), and that the duration of those punished is eternal.

We believe that God has made a way of escape from this place. "For God so loved the world, that he gave his only begotten Son, that whosoever believeth in him should not perish, but have everlasting life" (John 3:16). God does not want anyone to go to hell. The Lord is ". . . not willing that any should perish, but that all should come to repentance." (2 Peter 3:9).

DISCUSSION QUESTIONS

1. What is the purpose of the Judgment Seat of Christ?
2. Is the Judgment Seat of Christ for Christians only?
3. When will the wicked be judged?
4. Is the lake of fire literal?
5. Is hell eternal?
6. Will you have your senses in hell?
7. How can one escape hell?
8. Does God want men to go to hell?
9. Who will be judged at the Great White Throne Judgment?
10. Are you ready to be judged?

BOOKS RECOMMENDED FOR STUDY

Brewster, P. S. *Pentecostal Doctrine.* Gloucestershire, England: P. S. Brewster, 1976.

Ford, W. Herschel. *Simple Sermons on the Great Christian Doctrines.* Nashville: Broadman Press, 1951.

Simple Sermons on Heaven, Hell and Judgment. Grand Rapids: Zondervan Publishing House, 1969.

Pendleton, James M. *Christian Doctrines.* Philadelphia: The Judson Press, 1960.

CHAPTER 13

TITHES

W e recognize the Scriptural duty of all our people, as well as ministers, to pay tithes as unto the Lord (Hebrews 7:8). Tithes should be used for the support of the active ministry and for the propagation of the Gospel and work of the Lord in general and not given to charity or used for any other purposes (Malachi 3:7-11; Hebrews 7:2; 1 Corinthians 9:7-11; 16:2).

TITHING IN THE OLD TESTAMENT

Tithing Before the Law

The first offering mentioned in the Bible is that of Cain and Abel. In this text Abel's offering was accepted, but Cain's was rejected. "And in the process of time it came to pass, that Cain brought of the fruit of the ground an offering unto the Lord. And Abel, he also brought of the firstlings of his flock and of the fat thereof. And the Lord had respect unto Abel and to his offering: But unto Cain and to his offering he had not respect. And Cain was very wroth, and his countenance fell. And the Lord said unto Cain, Why art thou wroth: and why is thy countenance fallen? If thou doest well, shalt thou not be accepted? and if thou doest not well, sin lieth at the door. And unto thee shall be his desire, and thou shalt rule over him" (Genesis 4:3-7).

Why was Cain's offering rejected? The text does not make it clear. Early Christian writers connected the rejection of Cain's offering with tithing. Tertullian, for instance, in the third century wrote that God rejected the sacrifice of Cain, because what he offered he did not rightly divide.

A careful English writer, D. W. Thompson says concerning this passage: "So strongly has this view impressed some of the Church that in this history of the two brothers they find the first reference to the tithe, and in the Council of Seville, held about 590 A.D., a canon was passed which reads, 'If anyone does not tithe everything ... let the curses which God inflicted upon Cain for not rightly tithing, be heaped upon him" (Salstrand, p. 19).

We cannot be absolutely certain whether it was the tithe or not in this account in Genesis, chapter four, but the evidence shows that many of the early Church fathers believed it referred to the tithe.

The tithe is first mentioned when Abraham gave tithes to Melchizedek. "And Melchizedek king of Salem brought forth bread and wine: and he was the priest of the most high God. And he blessed him, and said, Blessed be Abram of the most high God, possessor of heaven and earth: And blessed be the most high God, which hath delivered thine enemies into thy hand. And he gave him tithes of all" (Genesis 14:18-20). This mentioning of tithe was seven hundred years before the law was given. We are not informed why Abraham gave tithes to Melchizedek. We are not told in previous chapters that God had commanded him to do so, but the fact he did so clearly denotes that he was acting in accordance with God's will and that he was carrying out His revealed mind.

Jacob makes a vow to God at Bethel. This was five hundred years before the law was given. "And Jacob vowed a vow, saying, If God will be with me, and will keep me in this way that I go, and will give me bread to eat, and raiment to put on, So that I come again to my father's house in peace; then shall the Lord be my God: And this stone, which I have set for a pillar, shall be God's house: and of all that thou shalt give me I will surely give the tenth unto thee" (Genesis 28:20- 22).

Jacob thought nothing would meet the approval of God as would giving Him a tenth of all God would bestow upon him. He can think of no stronger seal with which to bind himself to God than to vow to give him a tenth. In this connection it is well to ask, "Why did Jacob vow to pay a tenth? Why did he not choose the fifth, or ninth, or some other proportion? It appears as it did with Abraham that tithing was already established.

The Tithe Under the Law

The tithe is holy unto the Lord. This is to say that it does not belong to us. It is set apart for holy use, the tithe is the Lord's. "And all the tithe of the land, whether of the seed of the land, or of the fruit of the tree, is the Lord's: it is holy unto the Lord. And if a man will at all redeem aught of his tithes, he shall add thereto the fifth part thereof. And concerning the tithe of the herd, or of the flock, even of whatsoever passeth under the rod, the tenth shall be holy unto the Lord" (Leviticus 27:30-32).

The Levitical tithe was for the support of the Levites. "And the Lord spake unto Moses, saying, Thus speak unto the Levites, and say unto them, When ye take of the children of Israel the tithes which I have given you from them for your inheritance, then ye shall offer up a heave offering of it for the Lord, even a tenth part of the tithe" (Numbers 18:25, 26).The Levites had no inheritance in the land. The tithe of all the other tribes was their inheritance. It was not left to the whims of the people or how they "felt led" to give. They were to tithe!

The Results of Israel's Tithing

In the study of God's dealing with Israel, we note that when they obeyed God's command, they were blessed. When they became disobedient, God withheld His blessings.

There is a story in 2 Chronicles, chapters twenty-nine and thirty, of a revival in the days of Hezekiah. They turned to God in repentance and destroyed their idols. In chapter thirty-one is given the response of the people. "Moreover he commanded the people that dwelt in Jerusalem to give the portion of the priests and the Levites, that they might be encouraged in the law of the Lord. And as soon as the commandment came abroad, the children of Israel brought in abundance the first fruits of corn, wine, and oil, and honey, and of all the increase of the field; and the tithe of all things brought they in abundantly" (2 Chronicles 31:4, 5).

Hezekiah did that which was good and right in keeping the commandments of the Lord. "And in every work that he began in the service of the house of God, and in the law, and in the commandments, to seek his God, he did it with all his heart, and prospered" (2 Chronicles 31:21).

The same happens in Nehemiah, chapter ten, as a result of Israel's turning back to God in repentance. "Also the firstborn of our sons, and of our cattle, as it is written in the law, and the firstlings of our herds and of our flocks, to bring to the house of our God, unto the priests that minister in the house of our God: And that we should bring the first fruits of our dough, and our offerings, and the fruit of all manner of trees, of wine and of oil, unto the priests, to the chambers of the house of God; and the tithes of our ground unto the Levites, that the same Levites might have the tithes in all the cities of our tillage" (Nehemiah 10:36, 37).

In the days of Malachi, God charges His people with going astray; emphasizing they had not brought their tithe and offering to Him. "For I am the Lord, I change not; therefore ye sons of Jacob are not consumed. Even from the days of your fathers ye are gone away from mine ordinances, and have not kept them. Return unto me, and I will return unto you, saith the Lord of hosts. But ye said, Wherein shall we return? Will a man rob God? Yet ye have robbed me. But ye say, Wherein have we robbed thee? In tithes and offerings. Ye are cursed with a curse: for ye have robbed me, even this whole nation. Bring ye all the tithes into the storehouse, that there may be meat in mine house, and prove me now herewith, saith the Lord of hosts, if I will not open you the windows of heaven, and pour you out a blessing, that there shall not be room enough to receive it" (Malachi 3:6-10).

TITHE IN THE NEW TESTAMENT

Jesus Approves Tithing

The tithe was approved by Jesus when He spoke to the scribes and Pharisees. "Woe unto you, scribes and Pharisees, hypocrites! for ye pay tithe of mint and anise and cumin, and have omitted the weightier matters of the law, judgment, mercy, and faith: these ought ye to have done, and not to leave the other undone" (Matthew 23:23). Here Christ spoke of tithing in the term of duty, using the word "ought".

Tithing must have been practiced by Jesus; because He was raised in a pious Jewish home. They had to tithe! We know also that the Pharisees, who were meticulous in their tithing, and who would have loved to find fault with Christ, never once accused Him of failing to tithe. This is very significant. You can be assured if Jesus had not been a tither, the Pharisees would have condemned Him for not tithing.

The Teaching of Paul

The term "tithe" is not mentioned by Paul in his Epistles, except in Hebrews, which many attribute to him. Though the apostle does not use the term tithing as such, he does have a great deal to say about giving. And upon the subject of giving it was to be in a proportionate way. "Now concerning the collection for the saints, as I have given order to the churches of Galatia, even so do ye. Upon the first day of the week let every one of you lay by him in store, as God hath prospered him, that there be no gatherings when I come" (1 Corinthians 16:1, 2).

Arthur Pink states it this way: Now what does "laying by" imply? Certainly it signifies a definite predetermined act, rather than a spontaneous impulse, or just acting on the spur of the moment. Look at this again. "Upon the first day of the week let every one of you lay by him in store" (v. 2). Why are we told that? Why is it put that way? Why use such an expression as "lay by in store"? Clearly that language points us back to Malachi 3:10. "Bring ye all the tithes into the ..." Where? The "storehouse"! That is where the tithes were to be brought. "Bring ye all the tithes into the storehouse." Now what does God say here in Corinthians? "Upon the first day of the week let every one of you lay by him in store." There is a clear reference here to the terms of Malachi 3, but that is not all. Look at it again. "Let every one of you lay by him in store, as God hath prospered him." That signifies a definite proportion of your income. Not "let every one of you lay by him in store, as he feels led"; it does not say that, nor does it say "let every one of you lay by him in store as he feels moved by the Spirit"; no, indeed, it says nothing of the kind. It says, "Let every one, lay by him, as God hath prospered him": in a proportionate way, according to the percentage basis (pp. 13, 14). God's people are all to give the same proportion of their means and the only proportion that God has specified anywhere in His Word is that of the tenth, or "tithe."

In Hebrews, chapter seven, the apostle is showing the superiority of the priesthood of Christ over the priesthood of the Levites. Here we are told that Abraham paid tithe to Melchizedek, who was a type of Christ. Abraham the father of the faithful left us an example to follow. "And here men that die receive tithes; but there he receiveth them, of whom it is witnessed that he liveth. And as I may so say, Levi also, who receiveth tithes, paid tithes in Abraham" (Hebrews 7:8, 9). And the beautiful thing in connection with the Scripture is that the last time the tithe is mentioned in the Bible (here in Hebrews 7) it links the tithe directly with Christ Himself. All intermediaries are removed. In the Old Testament the tithes were brought to the priests, then carried into the storehouse, but in the final reference in Scripture, the tithe is linked directly with Christ, showing us that our obligations in the matter are concerned directly with the great Head of the Church.

The Use of Tithe

The tithe was a means of support to the Levites and the priestly system. There is a parallel between the tithe for the support of the Levites and that of the ministry of the Church. Matthew Henry states, "if the Jewish priesthood was maintained out of the holy things that were then offered, shall not Christ's ministers have a maintenance out of their ministry?" The practice of Christian tithing grows out of the Hebrew tradition and it is there that we discover its rich meanings. Tithing is found within the total context of Jewish law, a law which Jesus came not to destroy but to fulfill, and a law which Paul called sacred in its ability to convict us of sin, to prepare us for that which is to come, and to provide standards even in the presence of freedom. Thus, tithing has its roots in Hebrew faith, but is also watered and nurtured in the Word of the New Testament.

Paul, speaking of the support of the ministry says, "Do ye not know that they which minister about holy things live of the things of the temple? and they which wait at the altar are partakers with the altar?" (1 Corinthians 9:13). Tithe is not mentioned, but it is clearly implied in Paul's "Even so." "Even so hath the Lord ordained that they which preach the gospel should live of the gospel" (1 Corinthians 9:14).

THE BLESSING OF TITHING

"Bring ye all the tithes into the storehouse, that there may be meat in mine house, and prove me now herewith, saith the Lord of hosts, if I will not open you the windows of heaven, and pour you out a blessing, that there shall not be room enough to receive it" (Malachi 3:10).

God honors those who honor Him. And, God will not allow Himself to be any man's debtor. "Prove Me;" put God to the test. Try God out and see whether He is worthy of your confidence. He will open the windows of heaven and pour out blessings upon you. He will not only meet your needs, He will cause "the liberal soul to be made fat." It is ever thus when we faithfully honor God with our substance! John Bunyan wrote: "There was a man, Some called him mad; The more he gave, The more he had."

SUMMARY

We believe the doctrine of tithe is to be faithfully practiced by every Christian today — that this Scriptural teaching pre-dates the law — that it was incorporated into the law. We believe that Jesus in no way indicated that tithing was to be set aside; that Christ's statement "these ought ye to have done" (Matthew 23:23) should be accepted as what the Christian ought to do. They ought to tithe!

We believe that the use of the tithe was for the support of the priestly system, and that there is a parallel between the support of the Levites and the ministry today. Any church with ten families that will faithfully tithe can maintain a full-time pastor.

God has promised to bless those who tithe. He will rebuke the devourer for your sake. God will honor those who honor Him. This promise of an abundant outpouring has reference to temporal blessing. God will bless your income. If you are faithful to God, you can trust Him to supply all your needs.

DISCUSSION QUESTIONS

1. What is tithe?
2. What part of one's income should be tithed?
3. Do you feel that tithing was an established practice in Abraham's day?
4. Did Israel benefit from tithing?
5. What was the result when Israel withheld their tithe?
6. What do you feel is the New Testament's strongest point on tithe?
7. Should the minister receive the tithe?
8. Give a personal testimony of the blessing of tithing.
9. Do you believe that tithing is proportionate to all?
10. Can you expect God to bless you financially if you tithe?

BOOKS RECOMMENDED FOR STUDY

Pink, Arthur W. *Tithing.* Swengel, Pa.: Reiner Publications, [n.d.].

Salstrand, George A. E. *The Tithe.* Grand Rapids: Baker Book House, 1952.

Turnbull, Ralph G. *Baker's Dictionary Of Practical Theology.* Grand Rapids: Baker Book House, 1967.

CONCLUSION

In this series of the basic doctrines of our faith, it has been my desire to acquaint the student with the Scriptural teaching on each subject — to give the student a sure foundation in God's Word, that he may know what he believes and why he believes any of the doctrines taught in this series.

The author believes that as a result of this study, the Christian will be benefited in his daily walk. These truths, learned and applied, will make the Christian a better servant of his Lord and Savior.

After completing this series of lessons, the student should be able to share with his fellowman these wonderful truths.

TRIBUTE

Dr. Howard G. Tadlock's last sermon as pictured with notes taken by son(James G). Hebrews 12:1-3 (NLT) 1Therefore, since we are surrounded by such a huge crowd of witnesses to the life of faith, let us strip off every weight that slows us down, especially the sin that so easily trips us up. And let us run with endurance the race God has set before us. 2We do this by keeping our eyes on Jesus, the champion who initiates and perfects our faith. Because of the joy awaiting him, he endured the cross, disregarding its shame. Now he is seated in the place of honor beside God's throne. 3Think of all the hostility he endured from sinful people; then you won't become weary and give up. Hebrews 11:24(AMP.) ...though he died, yet through [this act of] faith he still speaks. Thanks dad, you left a legacy to believe that GOD IS FOR ME!!! ...and to all who believe!!!

Dad H.O.T. – 90th Birthday 11-16-17   Speak Visalia New Life Church

TEXT: Psalms 56:1-13
                9-11
        "God is For me" on your side
David was both Loved + hated by men.
ill. Joseph in prison → P.M. of Egypt
        Job
        Daniel – God's Favor + Acceptance
        Isreal – After Scattered ... 1946 A Nation
        Paul
ill.   1st Pastorate – Sultana, CA.
        Armona Bro. Wooten "In 6 mo's you'll
                                        be back"

        Built Orosi
        Woodbridge –
        Salinas   – Jim Bought Motor t.
        Norwalk   when I Lost
                             my Son To The
                             Evangelistic Field

        But God was For me.

BIBLIOGRAPHY

Adams, J. McKee. *Our Bible.* Nashville: Convention Press, 1937.

Bannerman, Rev. D. Douglas. *The Scripture Doctrine of the Church.* Grand Rapids: Baker Book House, 1976.

Brewster, P. S. *Pentecostal Doctrine.* Gloucestershire, England: P. S. Brewster, 1976.

Brumback, Carl. *God In Three Persons.* Cleveland: Pathway Press, 1959.

What Meaneth This? Springfield: Gospel Publishing House, 1947.

Chafer, Lewis Sperry. *Major Bible Themes.* Grand Rapids: Zondervan Publishing House, 1974.

Dickson, J. A. *Holy Bible,* An Analytical Indexed Edition. Chicago: John A. Dickson Publishing Co., 1950.

Fitzwater, P. B. *Christian Theology.* Grand Rapids: Wm. B. Eerdmans Publishing Company, 1948.

Ford, Herschel W. *Simple Sermons on the Great Christian Doctrines.* Nashville: Broadman Press, 1951.

Simple Sermons on Heaven, Hell and Judgment. Grand Rapids: Zondervan Publishing House, 1969.

Geisler, Norman L. and William E. Nix. *A General Introduction to the Bible.* Chicago: Moody Press, 1968.

Halley, Henry H. *Bible Handbook.* 22nd ed., Chicago: Halley, 1959.

Hertel Bible, New Encyclopedic Reference Edition. Nashville: Royal Publishers, Inc., 1971.

Hodge, A. A. *Outlines Of Theology.* Grand Rapids: Zondervan Publishing House, 1976.

Lockyer, Herbert. *All The Doctrines Of The Bible.* Grand Rapids: Zondervan Publishing House, 1977.

Matthew Henry's Commentary. VI, New York: Fleming H. Revell Company, [n.d.].

Nelson, P. C. *Bible Doctrines.* Springfield: Gospel Publishing House, 1971.

Pearlman, Myer. *Knowing The Doctrines Of The Bible.* Springfield: Gospel Publishing House, 1937.

Pendleton, James M. *Christian Doctrines.* Philadelphia: The Judson Press, 1960.

Pentecost, J. Dwight. *Things To Come.* Grand Rapids: Zondervan Publishing House, 1974.

Pink, Arthur W. *Tithing.* Swengel, Pa.: Reiner Publications, [n.d.].

Riggs, Ralph M. *The Spirit Himself.* Springfield: Gospel Publishing House, 1949.

Salstrand, George A. E. *The Tithe.* Grand Rapids: Baker Book House, 1952.

Smyth, J. Patterson. *How We Got Our Bible*. New York: Harper & Brothers Publishers, 1912.

Spence, H. D. M. and Joseph S. Exell., ed. *The Pulpit Commentary, I*. Grand Rapids: Wm. B. Eerdmans Publishing Co., [n.d.].

Strombeck, J. F. *First the Rapture*. Moline, Illinois: Strombeck Agency, Inc., 1951.

The Pentecostal Church of God. *Constitution and By-Laws*. Joplin, Missouri: Messenger Publishing House, 1977.

Torrey, R. A. *The Holy Spirit*. Old Tappan, New Jersey: Fleming H. Revell Company, 1927.

Turnbull, Ralph G. *Baker's Dictionary Of Practical Theology*. Grand Rapids: Baker Book House, 1967.

Webster's New Collegiate Dictionary. Springfield, Mass.: G. & C. Merriam Company, 1976.

Wiley, Orton H. *Christian Theology, II*. Kansas City, Missouri: Beacon Hill Press, 1952.

Wilson, Aaron M.. *Living Lessons*. Vol. 8, No. 4. Joplin, Missouri: Messenger Publishing House, 1976.

www.ingramcontent.com/pod-product-compliance
Lightning Source LLC
Chambersburg PA
CBHW070823110726
47973CB00003B/36